SOUTH EAST WALES

CHILDREN'S TRAILS

Published by Sigma Leisure - an imprint of Sigma Press, Stobart House, Pontyclerc, Penybanc Road, Ammanford, Carmarthenshire SA18 3HP.

British Library Cataloguing in Publication Data
A CIP record for this book is available from the British Library.

ISBN: 978-1-91075-818-2

Typesetting and Design by: Sigma Press, Ammanford.

Cover photographs: top: Guardian memorial in Six Bells © Blaenau Gwent Council; below: The Church Village Community Route © Rebecca Lees

Photographs: © Rebecca Lees unless stated otherwise.

Every effort has been made to fulfil requirements with regard to reproducing copyright material. The author and publisher will be glad to rectify any ommissions at the earliest opportunity

Maps: Sigma Press
Contains OS data © Crown copyright [and database right] 2016.

Printed by: Akcent Media Limited

SOUTH EAST WALES

CHILDREN'S TRAILS

Rebecca Lees

SIGMA Leisure

For Mum and Dad, who gave me my love of walking xx

Foreword

I always enjoy working and walking with Rebecca. She has a great sense of adventure and an in-depth knowledge of south Wales' best tourist spots and hidden trails. This lovely collection of children's walks should inspire families to get out into the great outdoors and join in Wales' big Year of Adventure – whatever the weather!

Derek Brockway
BBC weather presenter and meteorologist

Preface

"It isn't a walk; it's an adventure..."

2016 has been named the year of adventure in Wales, and about time too! The initiative, launched by the Welsh Government to promote the fantastic experiences and stunning countryside here, coincides with Wales being named by leading travel series Rough Guides as one of the world's top 10 countries to visit. This might be news to many but the only surprise to those of us lucky enough to live here is how long it's taken for the secret to get out!

Wales is fast becoming one of the UK's leading adventure destinations, thanks to attractions such as Europe's longest zip wire, the world's biggest underground trampoline, Bike Park Wales, Cardiff's International White Water Centre and more than 600 castles to explore. And that's before you get to the three National Parks and the 870-mile Wales Coast Path!

The trails in this book showcase 20 of our favourite areas in south east Wales. Some are along well-worn tracks already known to many, whilst others are tucked away in hidden corners just waiting to be discovered. Some can be done in just an hour or two and others can be explored as part of a longer day out in a particular area, with nearby attractions to be visited before or afterwards. Whether you've lived in Wales all your life or are here for the first time, hopefully there is plenty for families of all ages and abilities to enjoy.

Parents and carers everywhere, however, will know it's not always that easy to get children into the great outdoors. Rainy weather and the lure of computers and tablets can make 'going for a walk' something of a hard sell – but present it as an adventure and the wellies will be on before you know it! You don't even have to stick to walking, with several of the trails in this book also being suitable for bikes, trikes and scooters. You could set up an obstacle course, stage a treasure hunt or even have a silly walk contest if you want to – it doesn't matter as long as you're enjoying the fresh air and planning the next adventure!

There are so many benefits of walking, including better fitness levels and improved mental health for children and adults. It's pretty much free once you've invested in decent waterproofs and a good rucksack, provides valuable family time together and is a great way to learn about the environment, nature and history in a simple and relevant way. In fact, Ramblers Cymru has published a manifesto calling for Wales to be made the best country in the world for walkers, highlighting the importance of access to attractive open spaces and joined-up walking networks, as well as the benefits of walking for health and happiness.

And, perhaps best of all for parents, walking is quite simply a good way to get your kids to calm down! We've all been guilty of yelling at them when they are jumping off the furniture and refusing to go to bed, yet it's not really fair to demand exemplary behaviour of them if they've been stuck in a small space all day. But sometimes just an hour outside – jumping in puddles, throwing around armfuls of leaves, taking small risks and making their own decisions about which path to follow – is all it takes to burn off that extra energy and give everyone a good night's sleep!

As with South West Wales Children's Trails, the idea of this book is to give parents a starter for 10 in finding new places to explore, but the routes outlined are just suggestions and you may find completely different directions in which to head off! Just remember to stay safe and go well prepared, packing an OS maps, a compass and waterproofs on countryside and mountain walks and remembering the sun cream and water on warm days, even for a simple town stroll.

For each route we suggest a suitable minimum age and highlight whether the terrain is ok for pushchairs and wheelchairs, but please take these notes as a guide only. All children are different and some families with young ones will manage the more challenging trails quite easily, whilst some older children might prefer shorter versions of the long routes. Just trust your own judgement, check the weather before you set off and turn back if someone's not happy a mile in.

I hope you and your families enjoy these walks as much as we do and that they help you on your way to joining in Wales' year (and hopefully more years to come) of adventure! In writing this book I was helped by many people and groups who have long been working to promote Wales as an adventure centre to rival any, and as a result I'd like to warmly thank:

Rachel, Kyffin and Megan, Dave and Margaret Lees, Daniel Lock, Gina Gavigan, Mark Blackmore, Beth Jones, Alyson Tippings, Elly Hannigan-Popp, Ken Smith and Stewart Grey, as well as Ramblers Cymru, National Trust Wales, Newport Wetlands National Nature Reserve, RSPB Cymru, Garwnant Visitor Centre, Natural Resources Wales, Usk Conservation and Environmental Group, Cadw, Monmouthshire CC, Bridgend CBC, Merthyr Tydfil CBC, Newport City Council and Visit Cardiff.

Rebecca Lees
June 2016

Contents

Preface 6

1. Pen y Fan – the 'easy' way! Storey Arms, Brecon Beacons National Park 11
2. Pen y Fan – the 'hard' way! Pen y Fan Horseshoe, Brecon Beacons National Park 17
3. Geoparks and Giants Walk, Garwnant 23
4. Red Paths Ramble, Cyfarthfa, Merthyr Tydfil 29
5. The Guardian Trail, Six Bells, Abertillery 36
6. Goytre Wharf Wildlife Explorer, Llanover 42
7. Kymin Climb, Monmouth 48
8. The Tunnel Trail, Usk 55
9. Wetlands Wander, Nash, Newport 62
10. A Walk in the Woods, Lower Machen, Newport 68
11. On top of Old Smokey, Llanwonno, Pontypridd 75
12. Sunday Stroll, Church Village, Pontypridd 81
13. The Fairytale Trail, Castell Coch, Cardiff 87
14. Island Adventure, Flat Holm, Cardiff 94
15. To the Lighthouse, Vale of Glamorgan 103
16. The Tinkinswood Trail, Dyffryn, Vale of Glamorgan 110
17. A Day in the Dunes, Kenfig 117
18. Sand and Castles, Merthyr Mawr 124
19. Calon Lan Clamber, Blaengarw 130
20. The Keepers' Trail, Bryngarw Country Park, Bridgend 137

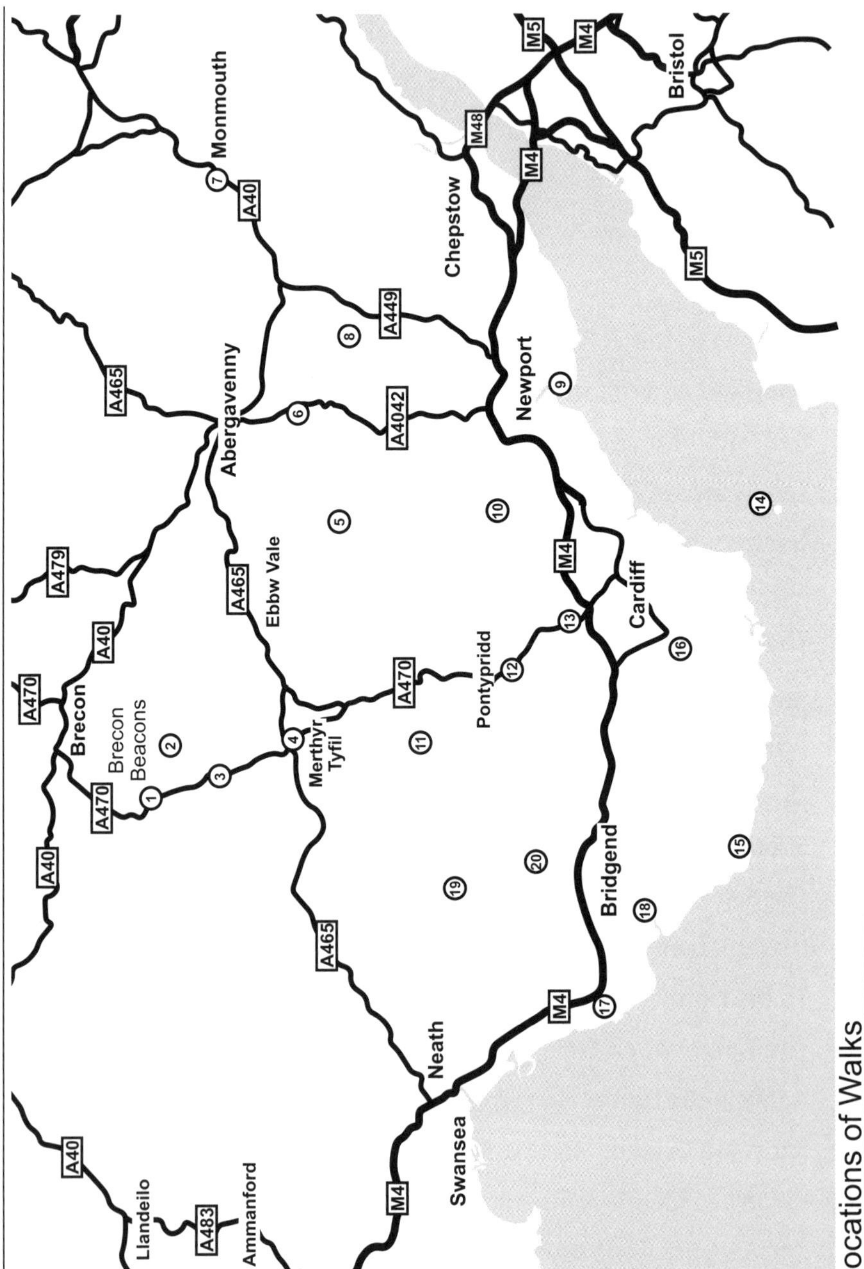

Locations of Walks

WALK 1

Pen y Fan – the 'easy' way!

Storey Arms, Brecon Beacons National Park

At 886m, or 2,907ft, Pen y Fan is the highest mountain in South Wales. It might not quite reach the Welsh '3000s' in height, but more than matches the North Wales peaks in terms of its spectacular setting and rewarding views, and is an accessible mountain for children to test their legs on before attempting longer, steeper climbs.

Pen y Fan means 'the top peak' and lies in the Central Beacons. It's mirrored by its secondary summit, Corn Du, which is Welsh for 'black horn', and the two peaks form a landmark sight above the A740 between Brecon and Merthyr Tydfil. There are several routes from various locations to the top of Pen y Fan, this path from Pont ar Daf being arguably the easiest to undertake with children.

This, of course, also makes it the most popular – so popular, in fact, that the world-famous peak even has its own Twitter account and Facebook page! On a sunny or crisp, snowy day, this route can attract literally hundreds of walkers, with car parks and lay-bys filling up first thing in the morning, so it's wise to factor in an early start... or think about choosing a less favourable day weather-wise! There is certainly something to be said for the sense of mystery and drama a misty day in the Beacons can evoke for children, but you might decide that the risk of climbing all the way to the summit and back without actually seeing the iconic twin peaks – as happened to us – isn't worth it!

Poor visibility also means that extra care needs to be taken and, although this route is described as the easier of the two Pen y Fan trails in this book, the word 'easy' is comparative. It remains a steep, challenging climb in a potentially dangerous environment, where the

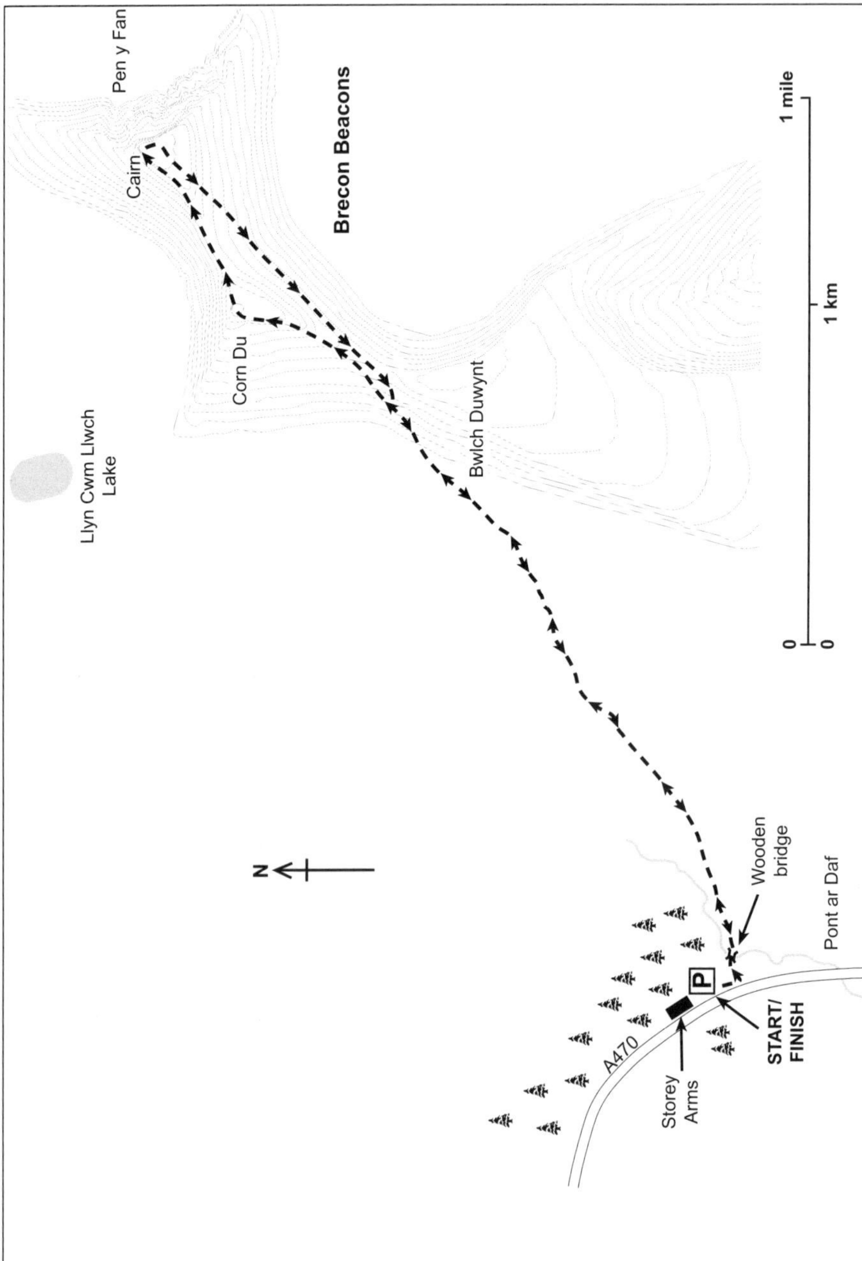

Pen y Fan
Cairn
Brecon Beacons
Corn Du
Bwlch Duwynt
Llyn Cwm Llwch Lake
N
0
1 mile
0
1 km
Wooden bridge
Pont ar Daf
P
START/ FINISH
Storey Arms
A470

weather can change extremely quickly and a wrong turn can be taken below the summit in mist or poor visibility. It's essential to be prepared, with sturdy shoes, warm and waterproof clothes, food and plenty of water, and to never let young children run ahead out of sight.

Approx. distance	**4 miles**
Approx. time	**2½ hours**
Starting point	**Pont ar Daf car park, Storey Arms, Powys** **Grid ref: SN 987 198**
Grading	**A steep climb along a well-defined track**
Suggested age	**6+**
Maps	**OS Explorer OL12; OS Landranger 160**

The Pont ar Daf car park is just south of the landmark Storey Arms, which used to be a pub and is now an outdoor education centre. The area around Pont ar Daf has recently been acquired by the National Trust, which is carrying out a major restoration project of the woodland following the spread of the tree disease *Phytophthora ramorum* across swathes of south Wales. The Trust is replanting the area with a 'wild' wood, which will be kinder to wildlife and more interesting for, and accessible to, visitors than the felled conifer plantation.

From the car park, facing the mountainside, go through the kissing gate near the information boards (with the bulk of the forest on the left) and cross the wooden bridge. The climb starts straight away, following the Beacons Way and passing a number of small, picturesque waterfalls.

Look out for the channels cutting across the footpath, which have been made to divert water away from the path and to prevent erosion. This part of the Beacons is 'common land' that used to be owned by the Eagle Star insurance company. Eagle Star gave it to the National Trust

The climb to Pen y Fan starts at Pont ar Daf

in 1965, to look after it for the nation, and you'll soon see a path-side plaque marking the occasion.

'Are we nearly there yet?'

The path climbs steadily for just over a mile, where it reaches a ridge called Bwlch Duwynt. This is Welsh for 'windy pass', and it's an apt name after the relative shelter of the mountain-side! Sharp gusts of wind can roar along here and the drops on either side are pretty steep, so it's wise to keep to the path.

Turn left and climb the wedge-shaped peak of Corn Du. The cairn (the pile of stones) on the summit stands on the site of a Bronze Age burial chamber, and the views from here are incredible. From the north, an alternative route to Corn Du passes the pretty Llyn Cwm Llwch lake visible from the peak, as well as an obelisk built more than 100 years ago in memory of a small boy called Tommy Jones, who sadly got lost in the mist.

From the cairn, bear right and pick up the path dropping sharply into the 'saddle' between Corn Du and Pen y Fan, where you'll need one last burst of energy for the final push to the summit of Pen y Fan! You might have to wait your turn, but taking a 'selfie' at the National Trust plaque is obligatory to mark your position as the highest person in south Wales!

The reservoir to the south is the Neuadd Reservoir, the starting point of the second – and harder! – Pen y Fan trail in this book. The next

The highest children in south Wales!

mountain along is called Cribyn, which, at 795m, is south Wales' third highest peak. Do you think you could climb all three mountains in one day, like lots of walkers do? It looks like a very hard task from here!

Return to the saddle and, instead of heading back across Corn Du, pick up the level footpath running under its summit. Walk back to Bwlch Duwynt, taking care not to overshoot the path downhill in misty weather, and retrace your steps back to Pont ar Daf.

WALK 2

Pen y Fan – the 'hard' way!

Pen y Fan Horseshoe

Brecon Beacons National Park

This is a long, strenuous walk that's not suitable for small children – or faint-hearted older ones! The walk starts with an extremely sharp climb, with two more to follow, and although the ridge sections in between are relatively easy-going, it's nevertheless a long and potentially tiring hike for which you do need to be well prepared.

Although not waymarked, the route is clear and easy to follow when visibility is good. Please don't underestimate the landscape, however, or the way in which it can look different very quickly when the weather changes. It would be foolish to attempt this route without an OS map, a compass, a well-packed rucksack and, of course, waterproofs and sturdy boots. It's essential to set off early enough to beat the fading light at the end of the day; the descent off Pen y Fan is steep and can be extremely tiring on the legs and, even then, there remains a good hike back to the car park.

Approx. distance	**6½ miles**
Approx. time	**4 to 5 hours**
Starting point	**Neuadd Reservoirs, Taf Fechan Forest** **Grid ref: SO 031 180**
Grading	**A very challenging route with several steep climbs**
Suggested age	**8+**
Maps	**OS Explorer OL12; OS Landranger 160**

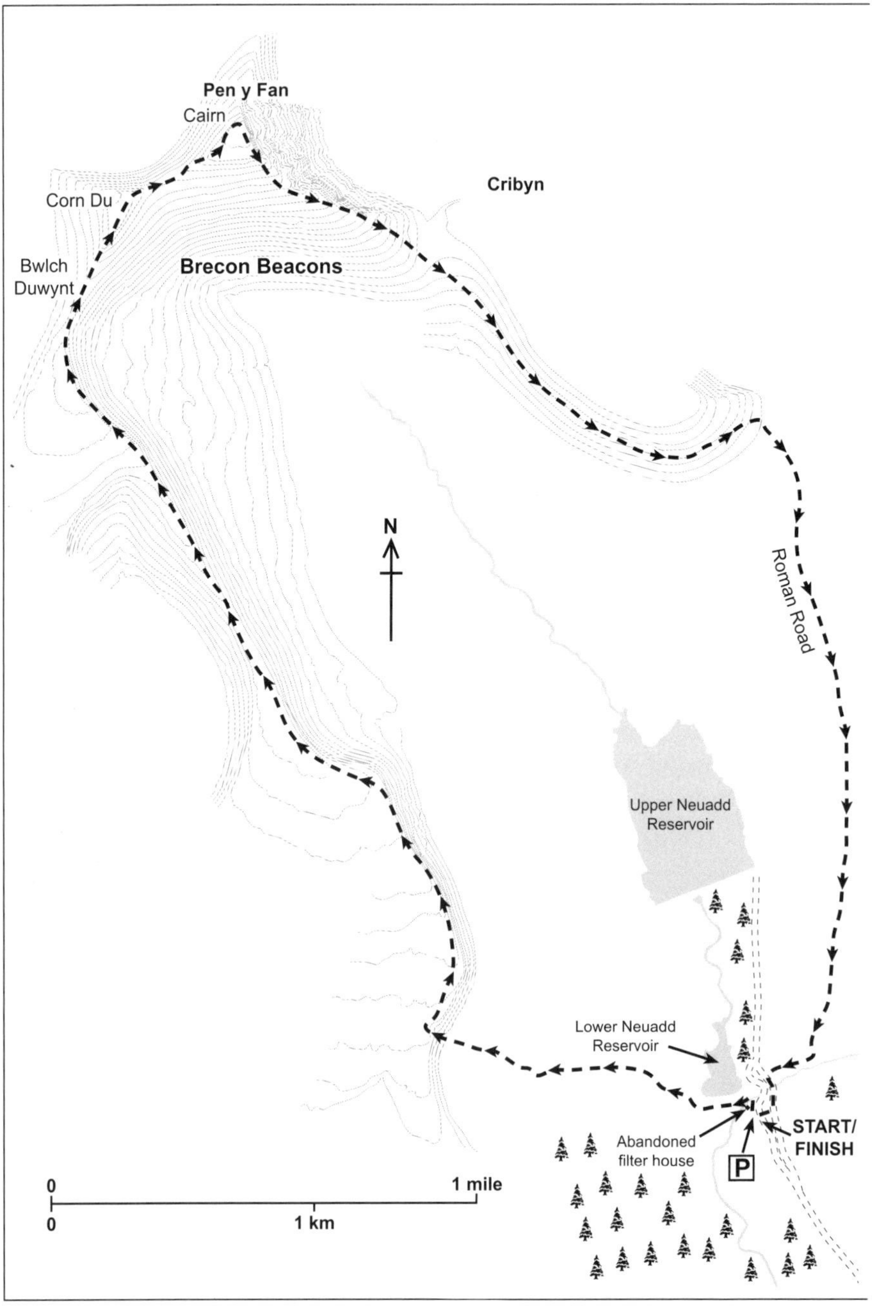
Pen y Fan
Cairn
Cribyn
Corn Du
Bwlch
Duwynt
Brecon Beacons
N
Roman Road
Upper Neuadd
Reservoir
Lower Neuadd
Reservoir
Abandoned
filter house
P
START/
FINISH
0
1 mile
0
1 km

That said, the Pen y Fan Horseshoe is an exhilarating trail for children and adults, with stunning views across the national park and south Wales. It's especially glorious on a crisp winter's day – just remember to pack the hot chocolate!

To reach the Neuadd Reservoirs, follow Vaynor Road from Merthyr Tydfil, passing the Pontsticill and Pentwyn reservoirs and continuing until the road ends at a metal metal barrier just south of the Reservoirs. The best spot to park is in a layby in front of the barrier, but this can fill up early in the morning, leaving as your only option the large forestry car park further back along the road (and adding a bit more mileage to your walk!).

Pen y Fan from the lower Neuadd Reservoir

From the barrier, follow the tarmac road, staying left at the fork. You'll soon reach an abandoned filter house at the foot of the lower reservoir, where the path dips downhill towards the cascade and then climbs back up onto the weir. The photo opportunities start here!

At the end of the weir, go through the metal gate and follow any one of the rough paths seen ahead. The ditch can be extremely muddy! We chose the path following the edge of the forestry, although others angle across the mountainside to join the ridge further along. Although relatively short, this is the steepest section of the trail and is an extremely tough haul! This is especially the case in snow, yet it's worth the effort in winter to see the intricate mini icefalls that freeze here in the shadow of the mountain.

There's a strong sense of achievement on reaching the ridge! An obelisk a couple of hundred yards to the left is worth a detour, but our route bears right, towards Corn Du and Pen y Fan. The ridge now runs north for a couple of miles, with envious views all around, and from here it's possible you'll see the RAF rescue helicopter circling on its training exercises.

The views along the ridge are stunning

As you near Corn Du – the first of the two peaks – the ridge path merges with another path approaching from the left. This is the popular 'Storey Arms' route from Pont ar Daf, outlined in Walk 1 and resembling something of a motorway on a clear summer's day! Cross the 'windy pass' to Corn Du, where you can either complete the climb onto the plateau or follow the footpath underneath the summit, into the 'saddle' between Corn Du and Pen y Fan. And then, with one final, short ascent, you're at the highest point in south Wales!

In the height of summer, you will probably have to queue to take your photo at the summit, so perhaps your time would be better spent enjoying the panoramic views across the Beacons, with Y Gyrn to the north and the Neuadd Reservoirs to the south. To continue the walk, pick up the path dropping steeply down the east side of the summit. Taken at a sensible pace, it's a safe path – if a little unforgiving on the knees! In winter, however, and particularly with children in tow, it's potentially treacherous, so you might prefer to return to the saddle,

Corn Du and Pen y Fan on a crisp winter's day

follow the lower path running horizontally below the peak and join the descending path a little further down.

Follow the path to the 'bwlch', or col, between Pen y Fan and Cribyn, the hefty pyramid of a mountain next along. Unfairly overlooked in favour of Pen y Fan, Cribyn is in fact another exciting climb and is, for many walkers, another 'nail' in the horseshoe to bag - but perhaps for us it's one to keep for another time!

The path now rounds the foot of Cribyn and meets a stony track said to be an old Roman road (although no archaeological evidence of this has been found!). Follow the track south, back towards and then parallel with the reservoir. Eventually the track draws level with the old filter house and forks at a mountainside stream. Follow the path downhill, towards the reservoir, and through the metal gate. Turn left along the gravel track, which we passed at the start of the walk and which takes you back to the layby and the car park.

WALK 3

Geoparks and Giants Walk

Garwnant, Merthyr Tydfil

At the southern gateway to the Brecon Beacons and five miles north of the busy town of Merthyr, Garwnant is one of those lovely places for those 'in the know'. Many people simply drive past it on their way up the A470 to Pen y Fan, without realising it's there... but, unfortunately for us, the number of those 'in the know' seems to be growing!

Garwnant's visitor centre has recently been refurbished and word has got out! The glass-fronted log café, with perfect views to the Llwyn-on

Humans are not the only visitors at Garwnant!

Reservoir, is usually busy, whilst the two play areas are brilliant, one for younger children and a low-ropes course for 8-15 year-olds.

Then there are the trails, for mountain bikers and walkers. The waymarked walking trails are perhaps more suitable for young families than energetic older children, the longest being only a couple of miles, but Garwnant is, nonetheless, a lovely introduction to the Beacons and the perfect place for a picnic and a stroll.

This trail combines the Animal Puzzle Trail, a half-mile waterside walk, with the Wern Walk, the two-mile trail taking you deeper into the forestry. Garwnant is managed by National Resources Wales - a new body replacing the former Forestry Commission Wales, Environment Agency Wales and the Countryside Council for Wales - and NRW has produced leaflets on each of the trails, which are available at the visitor centre.

Approx. distance	**2 miles**
Approx. time	**1½ hours**
Starting point	**Garwnant Visitor Centre, near Merthyr Tydfil Grid ref: SO 0031 1309**
Grading	**An easy forestry walk with a gradual climb**
Suggested age	**4+**
Maps	**OS Explorer OL12; OS Landranger 160 and 166**

From the car park, and with the visitor centre behind you, follow the road uphill and beyond the green metal barrier. The Animal Puzzle Trail contains ten beautifully carved creatures that live in the forest and along the river, with clues to each, and the first one is here! At the first sculpture, leave the track and follow the path on the left leading to the falls. It's a good place for a spot of paddling if you've worn your wellies!

Continue along the path, through the willow tunnel, and cross the river at the bridge. Here you can either follow the track uphill, away

There are lots of lovely creatures to see along the walk

from the river, to find all the characters in the Animal Puzzle Trail, or take the shortcut along the riverbank. Staying next to the river, cross another two bridges to return to the original riverbank, and climb the zigzags back to the main track.

From here, the Animal Puzzle Trail heads back to the car park. To take the longer walk, however, follow the wide track straight ahead (with the river behind you) and walk uphill between the trees. If you're feeling particularly adventurous, you can leave the track all together and pick out a path under the trees. It's quite dark in the forest but there are plenty of signs that people have been this this way before, such as the teepee we found made of branches and logs!

Garwnant is part of the Fforest Fawr Geopark, one of eight geoparks in the UK and 120 in the newly created UNESCO Global Geopark Network. A geopark is an area of geological importance, and parts of this one are 480 million years old! Throughout 2016, Fforest Fawr is

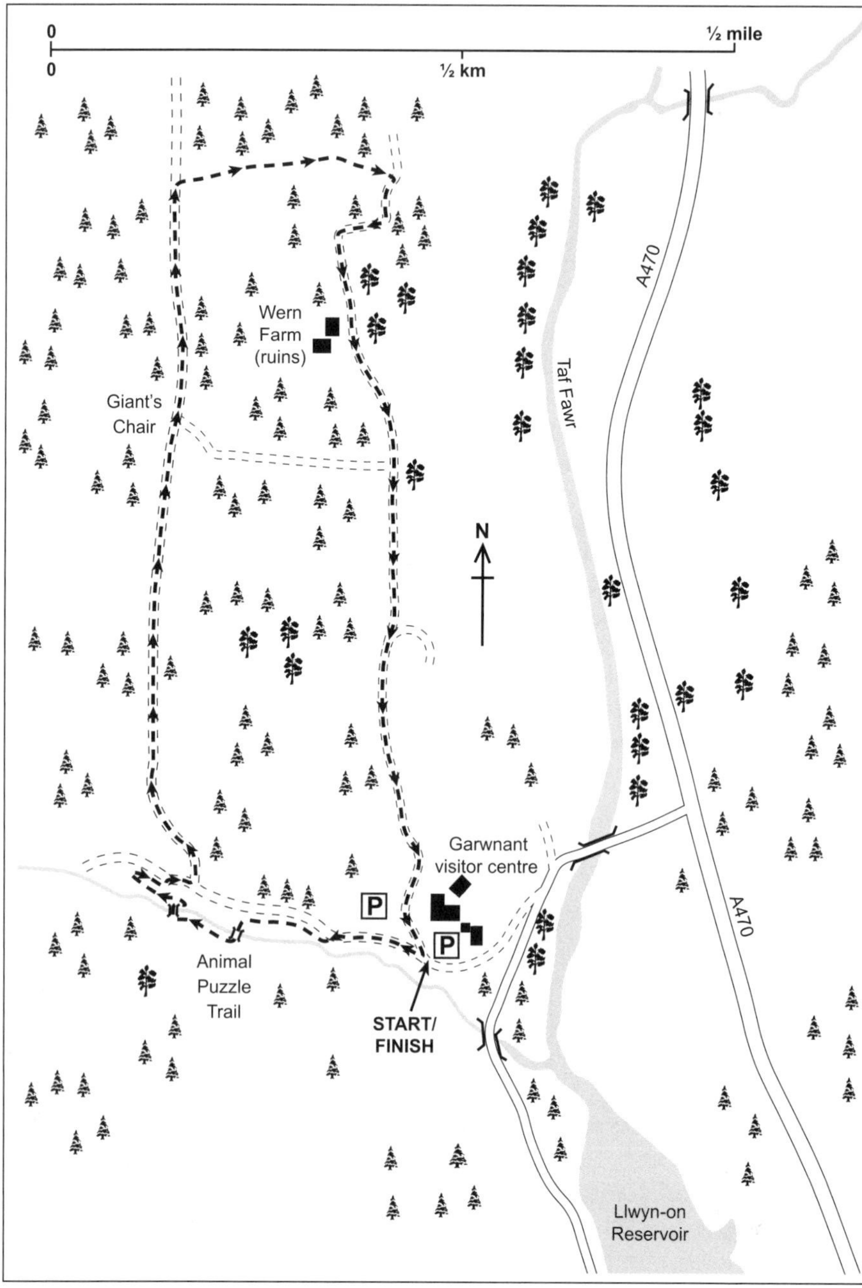
0
½ mile
0
½ km
N
Wern
Farm
(ruins)
Giant's
Chair
A470
Taf Fawr
Garwnant
visitor centre
P
P
Animal
Puzzle
Trail
START/
FINISH
A470
Llwyn-on
Reservoir

celebrating its tenth year as a geopark, so there has never been a better time to visit and explore.

Fforest Fawr stretches all the way from Merthyr to Llandovery in Carmarthenshire in a stunning landscape of hidden lakes, tumbling waterfalls and underground tunnels and caves. A number of trails further west in the geopark are explored in this book's pair, *South West Wales Children's Trails* (see page 144), including one around the sparkling Llyn y Fan Fach, which has the mysterious legend of the 'lady in the lake'!

The path continues to the brow of the hill, where you'll find a very unusual resting place! This huge wooden structure is the Giant's Chair and it takes some effort to climb onto it, but the views over the Beacons are worth it... if you're brave enough to risk the giant returning from the forest and finding you sitting in his seat! From the Giant's Chair, you can follow the path directly downhill, which leads

'Who's been sitting in my chair?'

back to the visitor centre, but the longer route continues north along the track until the next 'crossroads', less than a quarter of a mile ahead.

At the crossroads, follow the waymarkers downhill, along the grassy path, where the ruins of an old farmhouse called Wern Farm come into view. Pass Wern Farm and carry on, over the stream stepping stones and along the track to the green barrier. At the barrier turn right and walk uphill to arrive back at the visitor centre and car park.

There is still plenty to see and do before leaving Garwnant, with more carved characters to find in the clearing above the car park and a cosy pergola that's just right for rainy days.

WALK 4

Red Paths Ramble

Cyfarthfa Castle, Merthyr Tydfil

The red paths in the title are actually just one small part of this lovely ramble, which explores the grounds around Merthyr's historic Cyfarthfa Castle. But the newly restored red asphalt trails and the hidden features uncovered alongside them are certainly a highlight for the glimpse back in time they give into the life of the super-rich Crawshay family, whilst the rest of the park packs in a huge amount for families to do and see in a small but stunning space.

Cyfarthfa Castle was built almost 200 years ago at the height of the Industrial Revolution, which changed Merthyr from a rural village to the biggest town in Wales in less than 100 years. Life for the people employed in the vast ironworks was harsh, with terrible living conditions and a strong chance of getting a disease such as cholera or typhoid but, for the Crawshays, it was a very different story.

They built Cyfarthfa Castle with the money that poured in from their ironworks, which was said to be one of the biggest in the world. Originally the Crawshays lived in a large house on the site of the works but, wanting to get away from the noise and the smoke, they later chose this spot higher on the hill. The Crawshay responsible for having the castle built was William Crawshay II, who was married three times and had 13 children! The castle was built in just 12 months and is said to have 365 windows, one for every day of the year – although we didn't fancy counting to check!

Approx. distance	**2½ miles**
Approx. time	**1½ hours**
Starting point	**Cyfarthfa Park, Merthyr Tydfil** **Grid ref: SO 042 073**
Grading	**An easy stroll along woodland and tarmac**
Suggested age	**All ages, pushchair friendly**
Maps	**OS Explorer OL12; OS Landranger 160**

The walk starts in front of the castle, where a number of cannons are lined up. At the start of the 1800s, iron produced in the works was used to make cannons and cannonballs, and Cyfarthfa iron was so important in fighting France that Lord Nelson paid a visit to the works in 1802. Another person to visit Merthyr was the famous artist JMW Turner, who made a number of sketches of the town.

Cannonballs made from Cyfarthfa iron were used in the Napoleonic Wars

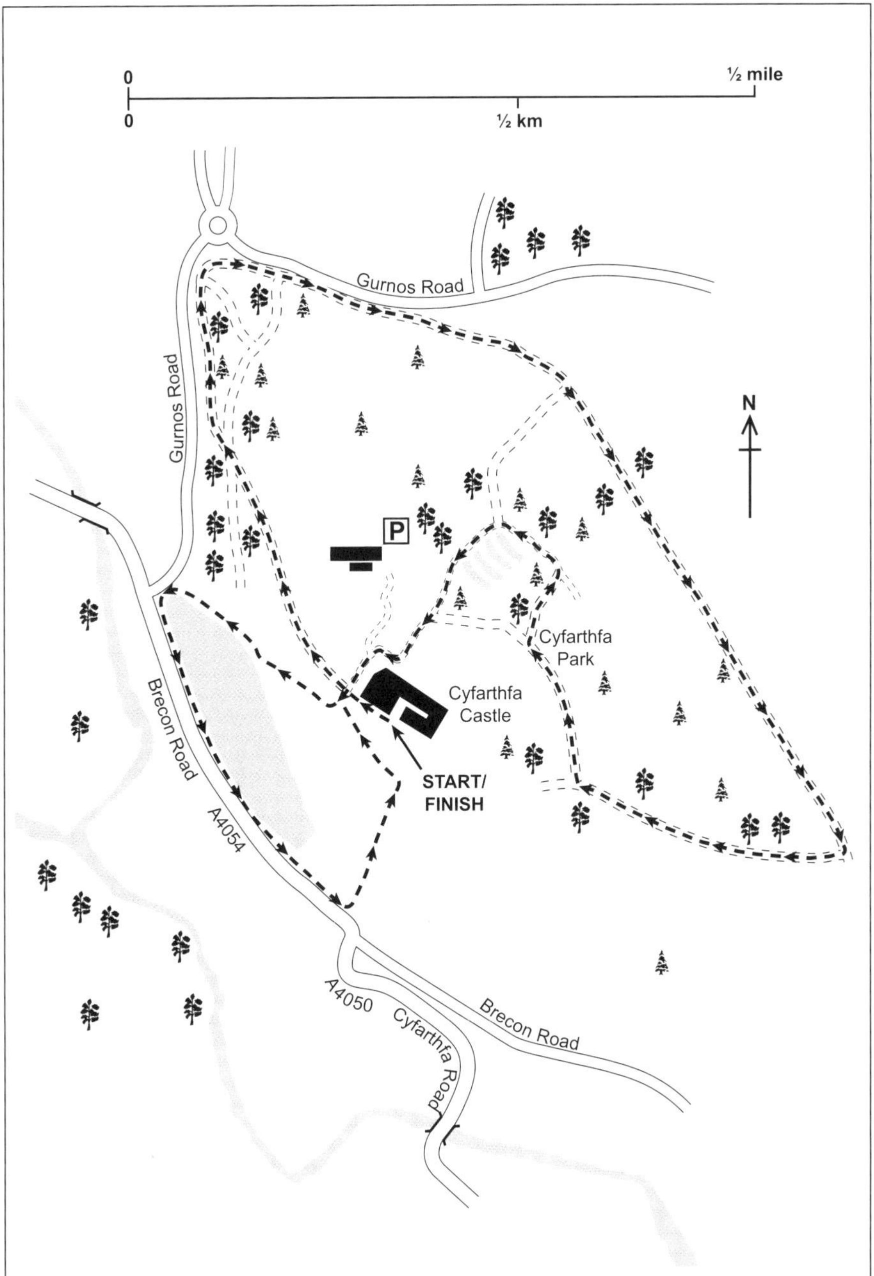

0
½ mile
0
½ km
N
Gurnos Road
Gurnos Road
P
Cyfarthfa Park
Cyfarthfa Castle
START/ FINISH
Brecon Road
A4054
A4050
Cyfarthfa Road
Brecon Road

Facing the castle, turn left and walk to the 'junction' at the corner of the building. Follow the path straight ahead into the woods and, at the first fork, keep left. Two centuries ago, a lot of hunting with dogs took place here and this is believed to have given the park its name, as 'cyfarthfa' is Welsh for 'barking place'.

The path reaches the very edge of the park and follows the railings around and upwards. Continue to the tarmac path and keep going straight ahead at the 'crossroads' until the brow of the hill. As the path starts to descend, there are beautiful views of the hills ahead, whilst to the right is a huge meadow, with a number of paths leading back to the castle if you want a shorter walk.

To do the full circuit, keep going downhill, passing the Wild Woodshop, to the rear park gates. Turn right (remaining inside the park) and walk until the castle is in sight again and the bandstand is ahead. On the right are two sign-posted paths, one leading to a

The play area is part of Cyfarthfa's regeneration

fabulous splash park and play area. The splash park is open only during the summer but the playground is open all year round and has imaginative equipment for toddlers through to teens, as well as the glass-fronted Canolfan Cyfarthfa café.

The other sign-posted path is... a red one! The vibrant asphalt was chosen to recreate the historic red colour of the paths, which, 200 years ago, were made from burnt colliery shale - also known as red ash. The work was carried out as part of a £3m project to regenerate Cyfarthfa, with the funding coming from the Heritage Lottery, the Welsh Government and other bodies. As well as returning the paths to the glory of the Crawshays' day, the new tracks had to be suitable for wheelchairs and buggies to make sure all visitors can access them, and they certainly do the job well!

Follow the red path uphill into the woods, with another entrance to the play park on the left hand side. At the fork in the path you can choose which way to go, arriving from both directions at four ponds that have also recently been restored. These feeder ponds helped keep the water in Cyfarthfa Lake at the right level and, in turn, the lake supplied water to the ironworks.

On the steep slope above the ponds is another interesting feature that was once a ruin hidden in the undergrowth and is now being restored, the domed icehouse. Icehouses were built close to water in the grounds of large houses as a way of keeping food cold in the days before fridges. Ice and snow would be tightly packed inside during winter and would remain frozen for many months, allowing meat and other goods to be safely stored.

The icehouse is also another reminder of just how different the lives of the Crawshay family were to that of their workers, who could be seen from the sumptuous castle as they toiled away in the ironworks below. In addition to the icehouse, Cyfarthfa had its own brewhouse, huge wine cellars and a number of hothouses used to grow grapes and pineapples - exotic fruits that the workers could only dream of tasting!

From the icehouse, return downhill to the front of the castle. Finish the walk with a loop of the lake by returning to the 'junction' you started from at the corner of the castle, following the drive downhill towards the exit gate and cutting across the lawn. The water in the lake was used to power huge machinery in the ironworks, travelling along a leat and across a bridge called Pont y Cafnau, which means 'bridge of the troughs' and still stands today.

Lionel the greyhound checks out the meaning of Cyfarthfa – 'the barking place'

The lake is now a lovely place to watch the swans and ducks, and test your fitness at the outdoor gym near the park's side entrance gate. Originally a boathouse stood on the shore; this is no longer here but instead Cyfarthfa now has its very own miniature railway, which takes passengers around the park on weekends and in the summer holidays. Run by volunteers, it has a full signal system and even goes through a 90ft tunnel!

Head up the main drive back to the castle, where there's a shop, the Popty tearoom and Cyfarthfa Castle Museum and Art Gallery. The museum is in the castle's beautifully restored Regency rooms and tells the story of Merthyr over the last 3,000 years, as well as housing a number of important paintings by Welsh artists including Penry Williams, who was known as Wales' answer to Turner.

In the museum you can also find out more about Rose Harriet, one of the daughters of Robert Thompson Crawshay, the grumpiest and most unpleasant member of the family! He was very interested in photography, which was still in its early days, and made poor Rose wear all kinds of strange clothes and pose for his photos! She also had to wash old-fashioned films and prints, which she hated as the chemicals stained her hands and made her embarrassed to show them. Rose finally got her own back though. He father had made her promise not to leave him until he died, but she ran off to get married – leading him to spitefully cut her children out of his will!

Other things to look out for in the park include a sensory garden and a number of greenhouses, which are used by members of the community and are open to visitors. They include a 'hydroponic' greenhouse, where plants are grown in water rather than in soil. In fact, Cyfarthfa Park has so much to see that you will probably still be wandering round hours after your walk has ended!

WALK 5

The Guardian Trail

Six Bells, Abertillery

This pretty trail follows the Ebbw Fach River along the valley floor at Six Bells and returns along a popular cycle path. It's never far from residential streets yet is secluded and peaceful, save for other families and dog walkers!

Deep in the heart of former coal mining country, Six Bells suffered a number of disasters, including a terrible accident in 1960 when 45 men died following an underground explosion. But the area once occupied by the mine has been given a new lease of life thanks to a dedicated

The beautiful Guardian memorial in Six Bells *Photo by Blaenau Gwent Council*

community team and an ambitious regeneration project. The beautiful 'Guardian' sculpture now dominates the landscape like a Valleys' Angel of the North, whilst otters, herons and frogs have made their home in the river and ponds.

Note that, although signposted from the A467, 'Guardian' is easy to drive past! From Aberbeeg Road (the A467), take Six Bells Road down to the valley floor. Where the road merges with Chapel Street, look out for Bethany Baptist Chapel and park in the adjacent car park. Ty Ebbw Fach is opposite, marked by a blue plaque.

Approx. distance	**2½ miles**
Approx. time	**1½ hours**
Starting point	**Ty Ebbw Fach, Six Bells** **Grid ref: SO 2208 0298**
Grading	**An easy, mainly level walk suitable for buggies**
Suggested age	**All ages**
Maps	**OS Explorer OL13; OS Landranger 161**

Although small, Ty Ebbw Fach is a must-visit, either before your walk - to stock up on leaflets about other trails in the area - or afterwards, for a warming cup of tea. The building used to be a pub called the Coach and Horses, but it was transformed into a café and heritage centre and opened by Prince Charles in 2011. The café is open daily, as well as for Sunday lunches, when it's essential to book in advance (note that snacks or hot drinks aren't served on Sundays).

Alongside the café is the Heritage Room, with visitor panels and old miners' lockers, which you can open up to find out what life was like for the miners. You can also learn about a Welsh artist called Valerie Ganz, who moved to Six Bells to study the miners and their families and painted them at work, as well as at choir practice and in chapel. Ty Ebbw Fach also houses community toilets, which are open to the public.

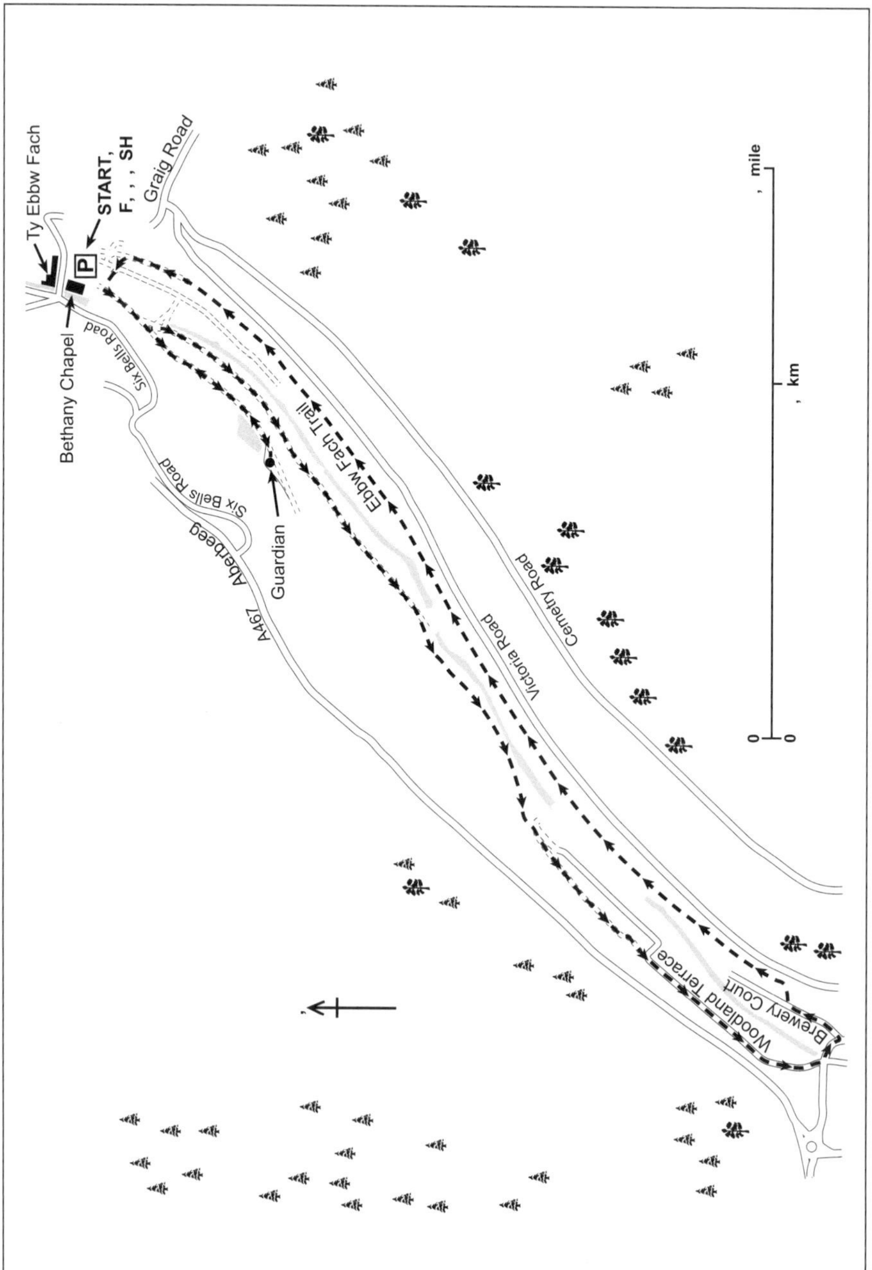

Ty Ebbw Fach
START,
F, , , SH
Graig Road
Bethany Chapel
Six Bells Road
Six Bells Road
Guardian
Aberbeeg
A467
Ebbw Fach Trail
Victoria Road
Cemetery Road
Woodland Terrace
Brewery Court
mile
km
0
0

From the car park, follow the tarmac path through Parc Arael Griffin to *Guardian*, which is 20m tall! It was made by a sculptor called Sebastien Boyesen and was unveiled in 2010 to mark 50 years since the Six Bells disaster. It's incredible up close and changes in appearance depending on the weather and the time of day, glowing red in the sun and turning into a black silhouette in fading light.

The land *Guardian* stands on was once the colliery site but no mining has taken place here for many years and, in 2013, Six Bells Local Nature Reserve was created. It has a number of habitats, such as grassland, scrubland and woodland, where bats nest and where you might hear or even see a cuckoo. And look out in the grass for slow worms!

From *Guardian*, return along the tarmac path until it branches off to the right, towards the river. Follow the riverside trail (with the river on the left) until reaching a gravel 'roundabout'. For a shorter walk, turn left and follow the path on the other side of the Ebbw Fach back to the car park. Otherwise, continue through the green metal gate and along the tarmac.

The path follows the river until reaching another gate in front of a row of terraced houses. Walk along the lane at the back of the houses and then join Woodland Terrace, continuing to the main road. There are some interesting buildings to look out for along the way, such as the old county police station. Can you see when it was built and what it's called today?

At the end of the street, with Brewery Terrace ahead, bear left past Aberbeeg Medical Centre and into Brewery Court. Walk a short distance past the houses until you reach the green bicycle gate onto the cycle path. This is the Ebbw Fach Trail, a good option for a longer day out on bikes as it links a number of green spaces between Llanhilleth and Brynmawr and passes interesting sights such as the quirky Roundhouses at Nantyglo.

Follow the trail through the woodland back to Ty Ebbw Fach. About halfway along the path forks at a wooden bench; by going left you can

A local nature reserve has taken over the derelict colliery *Photo by Blaenau Gwent Council*

There's a 'mine' of information to find on this trail!

return to the 'roundabout' on the far side of the bridge, whilst continuing straight ahead also leads back to the car park.

The Guardian Trail is a gentle option for families with young children, but those who want a more challenging hike might like to try Guardian Heights, a 5½ mile walk through the surrounding hillside forestry. Both walks are included in the Tyleri Trails series, nine scenic walks in the area devised by Blaenau Gwent Council and a local walking group called Tyleri Trekkers. A pocket-sized booklet of the walks is available in Ty Ebbw Fach.

WALK 6

Goytre Wharf Wildlife Explorer

Llanover

This tranquil trail follows a section of the Monmouth and Brecon Canal, or the 'Mon and Brec', as it's better known, with lots of history to find out about as well as nature and wildlife to spot. The route runs in a figure-of-eight with Goytre Wharf at the centre, a picturesque place where visitors can take a boat trip after their stroll, cycle along a national cycleway and enjoy the views from the waterside café.

Goytre Wharf is slightly further off the Abergavenny tourist track than the wharves at Govilon and Llanfoist and all the more peaceful for it,

The visitor centre at Goytre Wharf

although in its day it was a vital link in the chain between the Brecon Beacons and Newport. The Mon and Brec is 32 miles long and was built to carry goods like coal and iron to the docks, as well as bringing potatoes and wood back on return journeys. The canal was completed in 1812 and, when it officially opened, the bells of all the churches along it were rung in celebration.

This trail is one of a series created by Ramblers Cymru in partnership with the Canal & River Trust, which looks after most of the canals in Wales and England. The idea is to get families walking in and exploring the countryside and having fun in the great outdoors, whatever the weather, and the walks range from easy, mile-long strolls to longer, more challenging hikes aimed at older children. Find out more at **ramblers.org.uk/wales**

Approx. distance	**1.75 miles**
Approx. time	**1 hour**
Starting point	**Goytre Wharf, Llanover, Abergavenny** **Grid ref: SO 3134 0631**
Grading	**A gentle route along a canal towpath and open countryside**
Suggested age	**4+**
Maps	**OS Explorer OL13; OS Landranger 161**

Park in the pay and display car park and follow the short lane to the wharf and visitor centre. Walk into the wharf and take a look in the arches built into the large wall along one side. You should see some interesting characters! The wharf and these limekilns were built 200 years ago and the statues in the arches depict the limekiln workers of the day. It would have been a very busy place, with a weighing machine to measure lime and coal, a crane, stables and workshops full of activity.

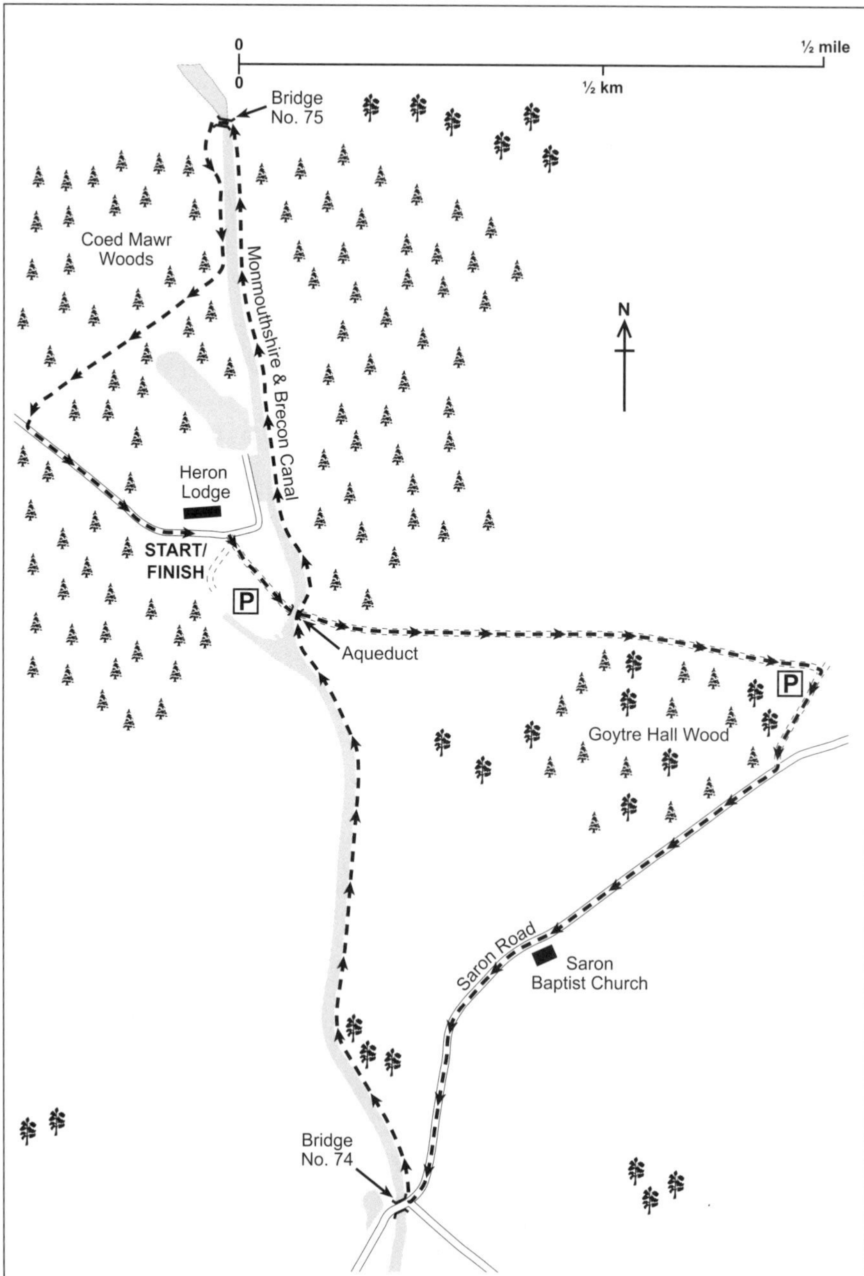
0
½ mile
0
½ km
Bridge
No. 75
Coed Mawr
Woods
Monmouthshire & Brecon Canal
N
Heron
Lodge
START/
FINISH
P
Aqueduct
P
Goytre Hall Wood
Saron Road
Saron
Baptist Church
Bridge
No. 74

These limekiln workers have been here a long time!

Pass Aqueduct Cottage and walk under the aqueduct, continuing straight ahead and away from the canal. Go through the metal gate and follow the footpath running along the edge of the field for about a quarter of a mile until it reaches Goytre Hall Wood, a small wood that has beautiful bluebell displays in spring. Follow the path to the small car park, where there are a few picnic tables and information about the 'Footsteps to Fitness' route, which our trail follows for part of the way and which starts from here. Did you know that walking 3,000 steps - about the distance of the first 'loop' of our figure of eight walk - burns roughly the number of calories in one can of cola?

From the car park, turn right and follow the lane around the wood and past Saron Baptist Church. Can you find out when it was built? Baptist churches tend to be simple buildings with baptisms taking place in the open air, and Saron was built with a purpose-made pool that took its water from a nearby stream.

The towpath along the ‘Mon + Brec’

Passing Saron, continue along the lane and join the towpath at bridge no. 74, heading upstream with the canal on your left. There are lots of ducks to see on the water as well as alder trees along the path, which thrive on the moisture from the canal. Follow the path for about a quarter of a mile to arrive back at Goytre Wharf, before continuing along the towpath (on the opposite side to the visitor centre) to complete the second half of the figure-of-eight.

Follow the path to bridge no. 75, searching for animal paw prints on the ground as you walk. If you're lucky you might see fox tracks, although, as foxes are shy creatures, they tend to disappear when people are about. And look out for other signs of 'life' – can you spot the large wooden snail?

At the bridge, cross over to the other side of the canal (the bridge is quite steep!) and go through the small gate on the left into Coed Mawr Woods, stopping at the information board to answer the 'true or false' questions on your way. The walk now follows a much shorter children's forestry trail and there are sculptures, dens and a story circle to find amongst the trees.

The path brings you back to the car park and the lane returning to the wharf, where you can try your hand at pond-dipping, with nets available from the boat shop, and find out more about the area's past. Goytre Wharf sits on the edge of the Blaenavon World Heritage Site, which has a great deal for families to do and see and is well worth factoring into your visit.

WALK 7
Kymin Climb
Monmouth

The climb to the Kymin from the historic town of Monmouth is not for the fainthearted! It's a long haul to the top of the landmark hill and the trail seems near vertical at times, whilst a section of the descent runs uneasily along a bumpy path. But it's an exciting route for kids who like to explore hidden tracks and efforts are rewarded with stunning views along most of the trail, particularly from the Kymin itself.

The Kymin can just about be seen from Wye Bridge!

Monmouth is an interesting town, with plenty of cafés, B&Bs and things to do. It's famous for its links with King Henry V, who was born in Monmouth and later became Prince of Wales. He fought and won the famous Battle of Agincourt in 1415 and, although it is remembered as a great English victory, in fact many of Henry's skilled archers were Welsh and marched all the way from from Monmouthshire to France. You can find out more about Henry V in the Shire Hall in Agincourt Square, where Monmouth's tourist information centre is also based.

Approx. distance	**3½ miles**
Approx. time	**3 hours**
Starting point	**Wye Bridge, Monmouth** **Grid ref: SO 5113 1280**
Grading	**A challenging and at times extremely steep climb through the countryside**
Suggested age	**6+**
Maps	**OS Explorer OL14; OS Landranger 161**

The walk starts from the Wye Bridge, which is on the other side of the busy A40 road from Monmouth town centre. It's safest to park in one of the several car parks in the town and walk through the underpass beneath the A40 to reach the Wye Bridge safely. From here, the white Round Tower of the Kymin is already visible – although it seems very small in the distance!

Cross the bridge and follow the A466 up to and over the mini roundabout, passing Redbrook Road on the right. At the next mini roundabout, turn right into Wyesham Road and start the long, slow climb uphill. As you round the bend, the Round Tower again comes into view. Walk past Kymin View Primary School and keep going until the houses peter out and the road becomes a country lane. Look out for Wyesham Lane on the left, tucked away by Springfield – it's easy to walk past.

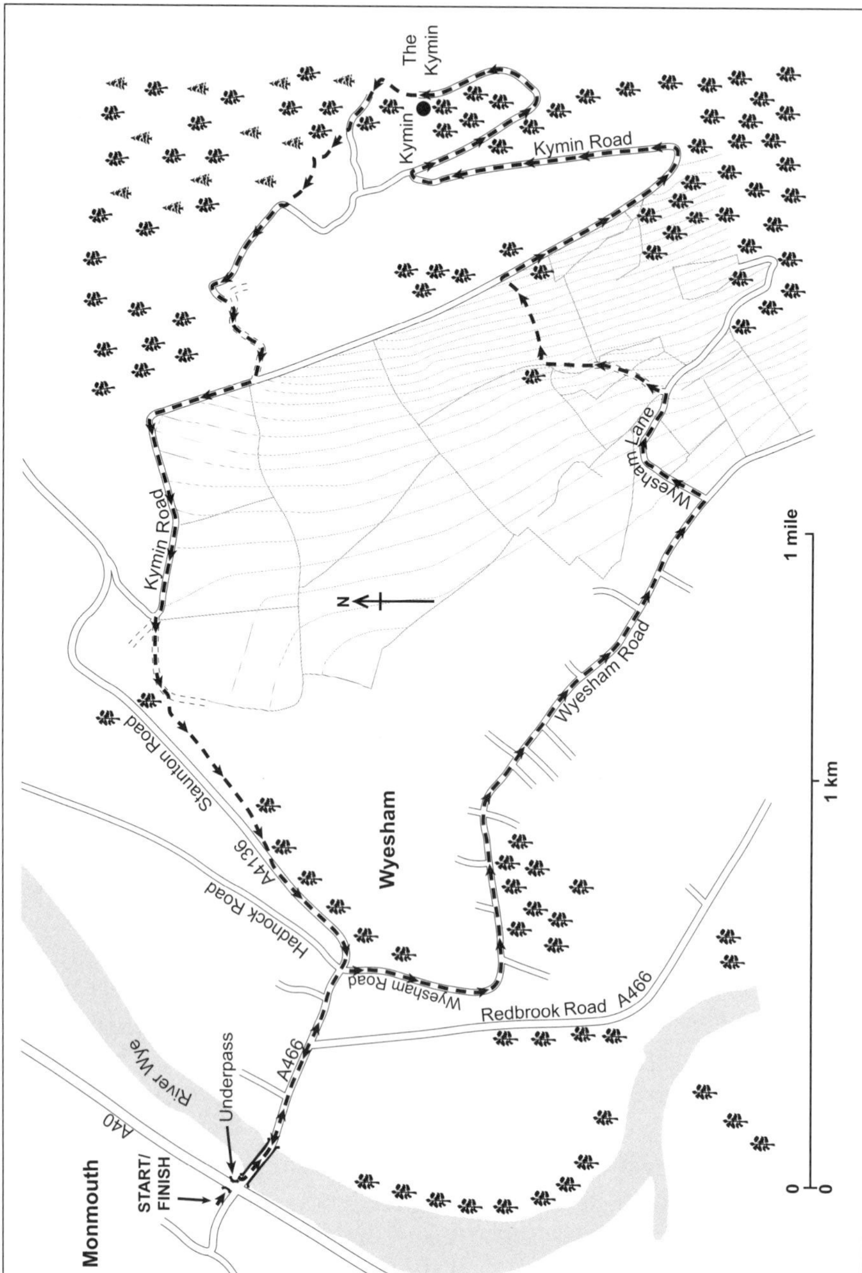

Monmouth
START/ FINISH
Underpass
A40
River Wye
A466
Redbrook Road A466
Wyesham Road
Hadnock Road
A4136
Staunton Road
Wyesham
Wyesham Road
Wyesham Lane
Kymin Road
Kymin Road
Kymin
The Kymin
N
0
0
1 km
1 mile

Now for the steep bit! The lane passes some pretty cottages and reaches a large house, behind which a wooden signpost points towards the Kymin through the woods (leaving the tarmac lane). The path soon reaches a stile, which emerges into a small clearing before the path continues uphill, back into the trees.

Crossing a second stile, it seems at first as though the options are either left or right – but we're going straight up! The path is hard to pick out, so look overhead and follow the telegraph wires. The footpath traces the line of the wires past the first and second telegraph poles, and then veers away at the third pole, continuing the extremely steep climb. The ground becomes rocky as it dips back between the trees to another stile, which leads to Kymin Road and, thankfully, a gentler stretch!

Turn right along Kymin Road and follow the horseshoe bends as the road zigzags uphill. Just past the second bend is the sign for the Kymin, which also shows the opening and closing times of the grounds. The lane makes a third U-turn and from here it's a short stroll to the visitor car park and information board.

From the car park, head for the white building you can see through the trees. This is the Naval Temple, which was built in 1800 to celebrate Lord Nelson's victory at the Battle of the Nile. He visited the temple in 1802, as part of a grand tour of south Wales, and was said to be very impressed with it! Lord Nelson had lost the sight in one eye at an earlier battle and a glass eye said to be his is on display in Monmouth Museum – but it's actually a fake! You can find out lots more about Nelson in the museum, which is also known as the Nelson Museum and Local History Centre and is in the Market Hall, Priory Street, just around the corner from Shire Hall.

A short stroll on from the Naval Temple is the Round House, the landmark white tower that can be seen for miles around. It was built more than 200 years ago by a group of local gentleman who met on top of the hill for weekly picnics and decided they needed a shelter for rainy days. The quirky Round House, complete with a banqueting

The views from the Round House are worth the climb
Photo used with kind permission of National Trust Wales

hall and kitchen, is what they came up with, and today it's open on certain days to give visitors a 'taste' of what it might have been like to eat a lavish meal here!

During the 1800s, picnics became more and more popular across Britain, and the Kymin has been a favourite picnicking spot ever since. It's hardly surprising, given the views all around! Looking in the direction of Monmouth, the pointy mountain you can see in the distance is Sugar Loaf, and on a very clear day you can see Pen y Fan as well.

The Kymin is run by the National Trust, which suggests its own walks from the Round House. You can ask staff about good routes through the grounds or visit the website to find out more. Lawn games such as giant Jenga, croquet and darts can also be hired and events run throughout the year.

To return to Monmouth, continue past the Round House to the wooden signpost and follow the path left, through the trees. This is part of the Offa's Dyke Path, a *really* long trail that follows the Wales-England border for 177 miles! Luckily we're not going that far although you will need a bit of energy to tackle the next bit, as, sometimes, going down can be harder than going up!

At the next signpost, bear right and continue to the wooden kissing gate leading into the lane. Keep going downhill past the paddocks; about halfway down, the Offa's Dyke Path bears into the paddocks and a sign clearly shows which side of the field walkers should keep to. You can take this path or, alternatively, continue along the tarmac to the 'junction' between two properties, with two green public footpath signs.

Look between the gap in the hedge for the yellow waymarker leading down the steps. Follow this thin path for a few paces then take the

Teddy bears' picnics have been held at the Kymin!
Photo by Sara Szwer / National Trust Wales

right hand option, which heads downhill and along more steps between two cottages, one of them called Fernbank. This section of the trail is steep, bumpy, narrow and, in places, rather overgrown. But it's also a good section for explorers who like to get off the beaten track and don't mind the mud!

The footpath eventually reaches Kymin Road again, via a flight of steps next to Number Five. Follow the road right, to the bend and past the entrance into Garth Woods. This is where the alternative route, the Offa's Dyke Path from the paddocks, reaches Kymin Road.

Walk downhill until Kymin Road forks back on itself. Don't continue around the bend but take the track straight ahead, which is a private road but allows public access for walkers. With the fruit orchard on your right, continue until the drive bears left and follow the Offa's Dyke footpath signposted ahead. This path runs gently downhill until reaching the road, with the Mayhill Hotel ahead. Follow the road back to the Wye Bridge starting point, where you can take a rest along the riverbank next to the rowing club before returning to the town centre.

WALK 8

The Tunnel Trail

Usk, Monmouthshire

This lovely trail is only short but packs a lot in, including a spooky railway tunnel and a quirky ruined castle perfect for firing young imaginations! Usk is such a pretty town that this trail should prove as enticing for adults as for children, with a string of independent shops, cafés and upmarket restaurants. The banks of the River Usk are ideal for picnics, whilst the river itself is a popular paddling spot in warm weather.

On the banks of the River Usk

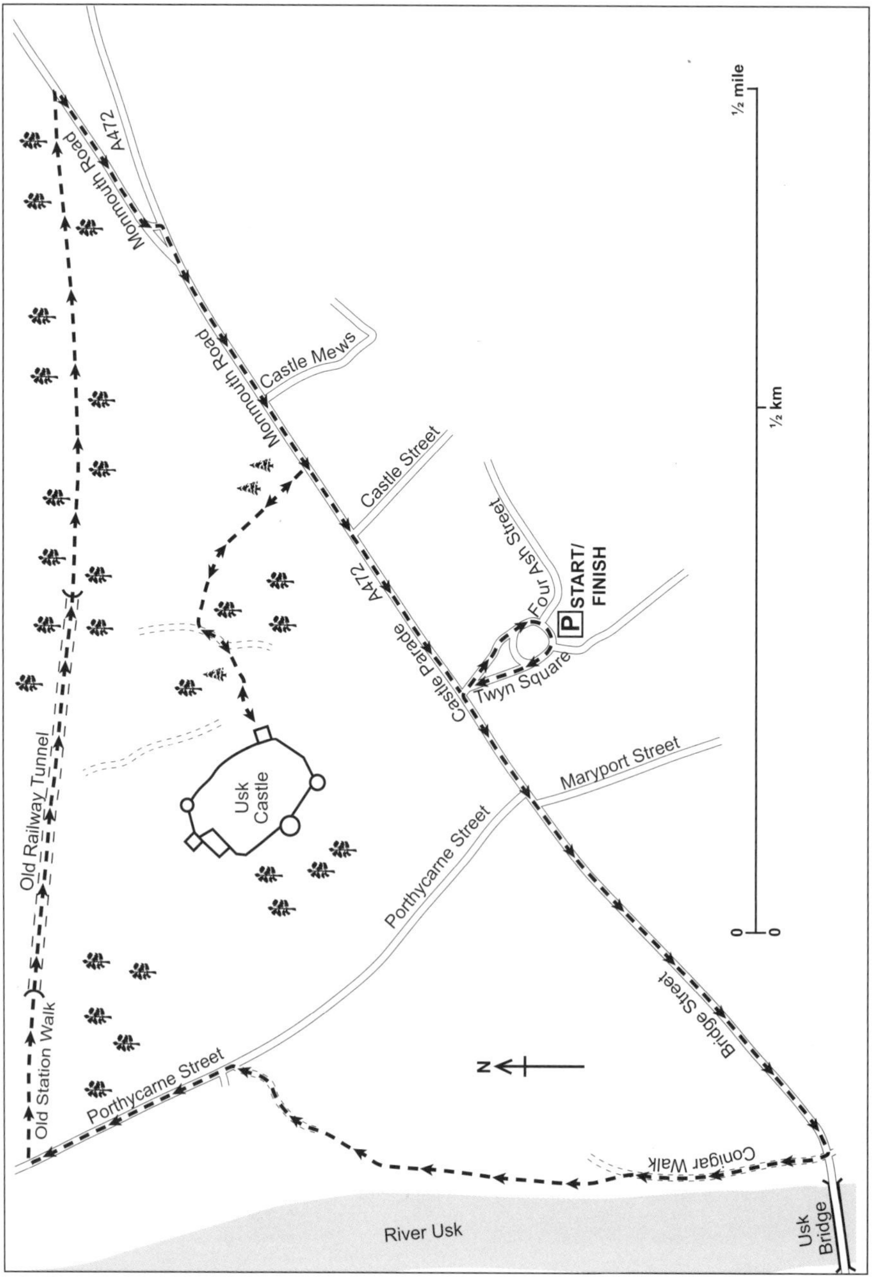

Monmouth Road
A472
Castle Mews
Monmouth Road
Castle Street
A472
Four Ash Street
START/
FINISH
P
Twyn Square
Castle Parade
Maryport Street
Usk
Castle
Old Railway Tunnel
Old Station Walk
Porthycarne Street
Porthycarne Street
Bridge Street
Conigar Walk
River Usk
Usk
Bridge
N
½ mile
½ km
0
0

This level walk is relatively easy for young children but the disused railway line can be muddy in places and is hardgoing with a pram or pushchair. Before setting off, it's worth noting that the tunnel itself is several hundred yards long and becomes pretty dark in the middle, although not pitch black. Not only does the already uneven floor seem even bumpier in the gloom, it might prove a little too creepy for very young or easily frightened children – although many will love it!

The other thing to know about this trail is that in order to reach the end, you have to do some hard work along the way! There are a number of clues to solve as you go, but don't worry if you get stuck as the answers are at the end of the chapter.

Approx. distance	**1½ miles**
Approx. time	**1 hour**
Starting point	**The Square, Usk** **Grid ref: SO 3777 0089**
Grading	**An easy, level walk but with poor pushchair access in places**
Suggested age	**4+**
Maps	**OS Explorer OL14; OS Landranger 161**

The walk starts from Twyn Square, where the eye-catching old clock tower looks even more attractive surrounded by tubs of planted flowers. The town is very proud of its 'Usk in Bloom' competition, with green-fingered locals making the streets bright and cheerful with beautiful displays everywhere you look. It's possible to park at the (very) small car park in Twyn Square, in front of the clock tower but, if this is full, there's a much larger car park, as well as public toilets, next to nearby Usk Museum.

Cross Twyn Square, passing the clock tower, and turn left into Bridge Street.

1. *Carry on along the street*
And count the creatures said to leap!

Can you work it out? We'll give you a clue; you need to look along the right hand side of the street!

Continue all the way along the street to Usk Bridge, which was built more than 250 years ago. It was narrower in those days as there were no cars and the only traffic would have been horses and carts! Stay this side of the river and take a look around.

2. *The initials 'ER' are plain to see,*
But you wouldn't want to spend a night in me!

What am I? And what do the initials ER stand for?

Take the footpath on the right, away from the bridge and along the riverbank. You're now following Conigar Walk, an area that was used hundreds of years ago - but what for?

3. *With so many friends, we're never lonely,*
But just who lived inside this 'coney'?

Carry on along Conigar Walk, passing the first turning on the right and bearing left at the fork. The path heads slightly uphill, alongside a wooden fence, and then downhill, away from the river. Follow the narrow lane to Porthycarne Street, where the trail turns left along the pavement to the old railway bridge.

Cross the road and follow the tarmac path, the Old Station Walk, into the woods. The track winds around almost in a circle; ignore the first path on the right waymarked in yellow and continue around to reach the line of the old railway. To your right is a huge, dark railway tunnel - and we're going in!

The railway track has long gone and there are no trains whistling past to worry about; in fact, the only risk today comes from the regular

Enter the tunnel if you dare!

drips of water that tunnelswalkers are likely to feel landing on their heads! We found it best to stay in the middle of the tunnel, where the ground is slightly dryer than along the edges, but you still need to go carefully as it's very uneven.

The disused railway forms part of the Usk Nature Trail. On reaching the other end of the tunnel the path runs through the woods alongside a shallow leat, and it's a nice stretch along which to look for signs of nature in the water and on the embankment as you walk.

Before long the path reaches another, shorter, tunnel. This time we're not going through it but over it, via the steps to the left.

4. *This walk is popular, so we've heard,*
Named after a colourful, singing bird

Carry on to the clearing alongside Monmouth Road, where there's a handy bench in case you need a rest. Turning right, follow Monmouth

Road back towards Usk town centre. Very soon you'll reach the entrance to Usk Castle on the right – just head up the drive to the gateway!

5. *For this next clue, don't look down*
The king of every castle needs a ——-!

Usk Castle is very different to the posh stately homes you might have visited before! It's a ramshackle ruin and not large, but it's utterly charming and very easy to imagine full of medieval knights and ladies. It's privately owned and visitors are asked to make a donation in the box on their way in.

The castle is more than 800 years old and was built by a knight called William, whose wife had ten children! Although today Usk Castle looks as though it might fall down at any minute, it was actually a masterpiece, cleverly designed to keep out invaders.

Queen of the castle

It certainly did so in 1405, when supporters of the famous Welsh prince, Owain Glyndwr, tried to capture the castle in the Battle of Usk. They were defeated and 300 men were reported to have been captured and gruesomely beheaded in front of the castle walls! The battle also became known as the Battle of Pwll Melyn, as much of the fighting took place at the 'yellow pool' just north of the castle, where bones are said to have been discovered when the pond was cleaned out.

Hopefully the enemy won't attack you today but, nevertheless, visitors enter the castle at their own risk! A number of hidden creatures are lurking just around the corner - how many can you see?

If you've ever fancied staying in a castle, here's your chance - well, nearly! In the grounds is Usk Castle Knights Glamping, an encampment of ready-made, striped pavilions with comfortable beds and a shared kitchen and shower block, whilst campers can also pitch their own tents too. Castle Knights is open from April to September and it's advisable to book in advance.

From the castle - which, by the way, stands almost on top of the railway tunnel you've just walked through! - return to Monmouth Road. Turn right and back towards the town centre and Twyn Square. At the very end of the trail is a traditional fish n' chip shop and café, where we can vouch for a hearty and very well deserved tea after your adventures.

Answers!

Clue 1:	*The Three Salmons Hotel*
Clue 2:	*Usk Police Station. The initials 'ER' stand for Elizabeth Regina, after Queen Elizabeth II.*
Clue 3:	*Rabbits*
Clue 4:	*Bullfinch Walk*
Clue 5:	*Crown*

WALK 9
Wetlands Wander
Nash, Newport

The Newport Wetlands National Nature Reserve is one of those lovely locations in which to 'get away from it all' without going far! Lying between the Severn Estuary and the River Usk, it's just on the edge of the city of Newport and easy to reach from the M4, yet with refreshing coastal views and perfect peace – apart from the birdsong, of course! The reserve is owned and managed by Natural Resources Wales working in partnership with RSPB Cymru, Newport City Council and others for the benefit of wildlife and visitors.

A mute swan at Newport Wetlands National Nature Reserve
Photo by RSPB

Note that dogs are welcome on the permissive circular route but not within the reserve itself, so please call at the Newport Wetlands Visitor Centre for details. This trail starts on the permissive path but later enters the reserve, so one option for dog walkers is to go as far as the East Usk Lighthouse and then return the same way. For a much longer walk with dogs, you can continue along the Wales Coast Path and circle the reserve altogether, but this is about six miles in total and misses the chance to use the reserve bird hide and visit the play area.

Approx. distance	**3 miles**
Approx. time	**1½ hours**
Starting point	**Newport Wetlands National Nature Reserve, Nash, Newport** **Grid ref: ST 3346 8344**
Grading	**An easy, level walk suitable for pushchairs and wheelchairs**
Suggested age	**4+**
Maps	**OS Explorer 152; OS Landranger 171**

The walk starts from the car park although, before starting out, you may want to pop to the visitor centre a short distance inside the gate for maps and activity sheets. Facing the nature reserve from the car park, follow the path right, towards the power station, with its huge chimney looming ahead. The trail winds around the edge of the reserve between the power station and the thick, tall reed beds, which are home to many species of bird such as water rail and bearded tit. A number of paths lead into the nature reserve through the reed beds, but stick to the main path where, after about three quarters of a mile, the sea comes into view!

The land along this stretch of coast is covered in ash from the power station, but the reserve was established in 2000 to make up for the loss of habitat further along the coast when the Cardiff Bay Barrage was built. The reed beds were created and today the area is a pretty and peaceful sanctuary for birds.

Take a look to the far banks of the estuary where, on a clear day, you should be able to make out the West Usk Lighthouse. We are heading for its pair, the East Usk Lighthouse, which you might already be able to see above the reed beds. Carry on along the coast path to the

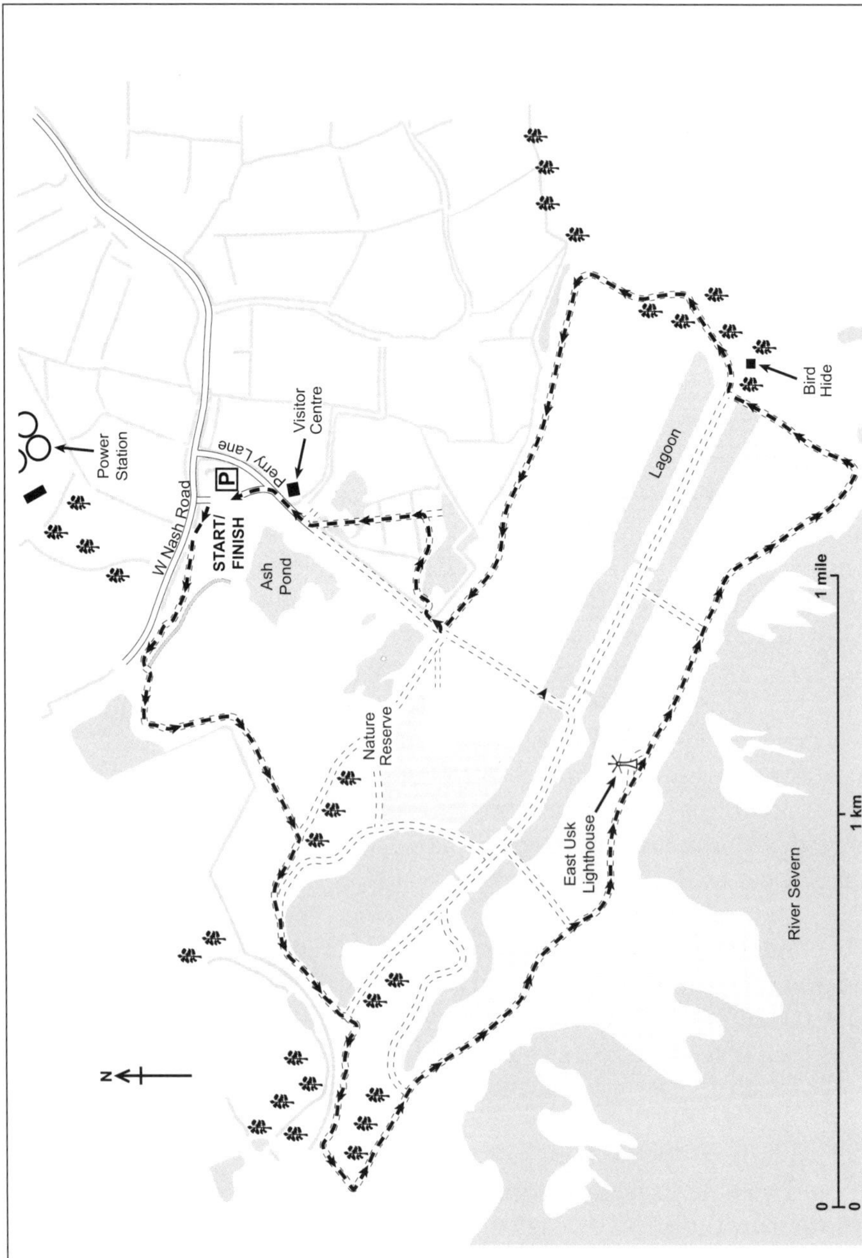
N
Power Station
W Nash Road
Perry Lane
Visitor Centre
START/ FINISH
Ash Pond
Lagoon
Bird Hide
Nature Reserve
East Usk Lighthouse
River Severn
0
1 mile
0
1 km

lighthouse. It's much smaller than Flat Holm and Nash Point lighthouses in walks 14 and 15! East Usk Lighthouse was built in 1893 by a man called Thomas Williams, who used his horse to drag the steel here from the nearby village of Nash! His family continued to keep the lighthouse for many years and it still works today, sending out two flashes every 10 seconds as a warning to ships in the estuary.

East Usk Lighthouse is on the 870-mile long Wales Coast Path

After a rest on the bench alongside the lighthouse, carry on along the coast path for about a third of a mile, where the path turns at a right angle and heads away from the sea. At the wooden signpost, the coast path continues but our trail carries on straight ahead, into the nature reserve. A short distance on is the bird hide, with a view across a wide lagoon all the way to the little lighthouse and the power station in the distance.

Take a look at the posters of birds on the hide wall and see if you can spot any on the water. The reserve is a winter home to a shy type of heron called the bittern, which is still under threat but is now being

The lighthouse beyond the reed bed *Photo by RSPB*

spotted more and more in Wales and England. Reed buntings also live here, as well as otters.

From the bird hide, continue along the path into a small wood. Newport Wetlands has a number of short trails from the visitor centre, and this is part of the woodland and estuary trail. Emerging from the woods, the trail now runs west again, back towards the visitor centre. The Wetlands are in the heart of the Gwent Levels, an area stretching all the way from the Severn Bridge to Cardiff that's very rich in wildlife, including dragonflies, water beetles and water voles.

At the 'crossroads', turn right towards the visitor centre - although before reaching the centre you might get side-tracked by the play area! It has an apt waterside theme and a clever replica of the East Usk Lighthouse (which doesn't seem that much smaller than the real thing!).

The visitor centre is well stocked with leaflets about birds and nature, for which you can make a donation in the RSPB robin collection box. There's also a large glass-fronted café with superb views across the reserve. The staff are very knowledgeable and helpful, and run activities in school holidays and on special occasions that are worth finding out about.

WALK 10

A Walk in the Woods

Lower Machen, Newport

This hilly woodland on the boundary between Newport and Caerphilly is a great place to burn off energy and play in the mud! It follows a section of the Rhymney River Circular Walk, a nine-mile hike through the lower Rhymney Valley that might appeal to older children. It is also Newport Council's Iron Bridge Walk and has been clearly waymarked, so you shouldn't get lost in the woods - unless you want to, of course!

Coed Craig Ruperra is a dense wood sitting in a crook of the Rhymney River. The name Ruperra originates from Rhiw'r Perrai - the hill of

It's uphill all the way to the Iron Age hill fort!

pear trees - and the wood was mentioned in the first records of the Ancient Woodlands in Wales as long ago as 1600. Today it's a peaceful place to spot birds and, if you're extremely lucky, dormice - although they are very shy creatures. Twenty years ago, they started to lose their habitat here as many trees were felled, but recently a number of special nest boxes have been placed in the trees to protect them. The woodland is owned by a local trust and is free to enter, but note that it's all about the nature here and there are no cafés or toilets!

The network of paths can get very muddy in wet weather and the combination of slippery sections and the gradient might mean this walk takes longer than your average three-mile stroll. The full circuit is perhaps too much of a trek for very small children, so a pleasant alternative is to reach Craig Ruperra, enjoy the views and then return the way you came.

Approx. distance	**3 miles**
Approx. time	**2½ hours**
Starting point	**Draethen, Lower Machen, Newport** **Grid ref: ST 2210 8732**
Grading	**A woodland walk with steep sections and uneven paths**
Suggested age	**5+**
Maps	**OS Explorer 152; OS Landranger 171**

The walk starts from the centre of the village of Draethen, where there is space to park on the roadside near a pub called the Hollybush. Alternatively, there is a large car park on the north west edge of the woodland, through which the trail later passes, so another option is to start from there and walk the 'last' section first.

If starting from the Hollybush, approach the pub and cross the stile to the right of the building to follow the footpath climbing uphill behind the pub, through the field towards the woods. If you have a dog it's worth noting that large dogs might not be able to get under

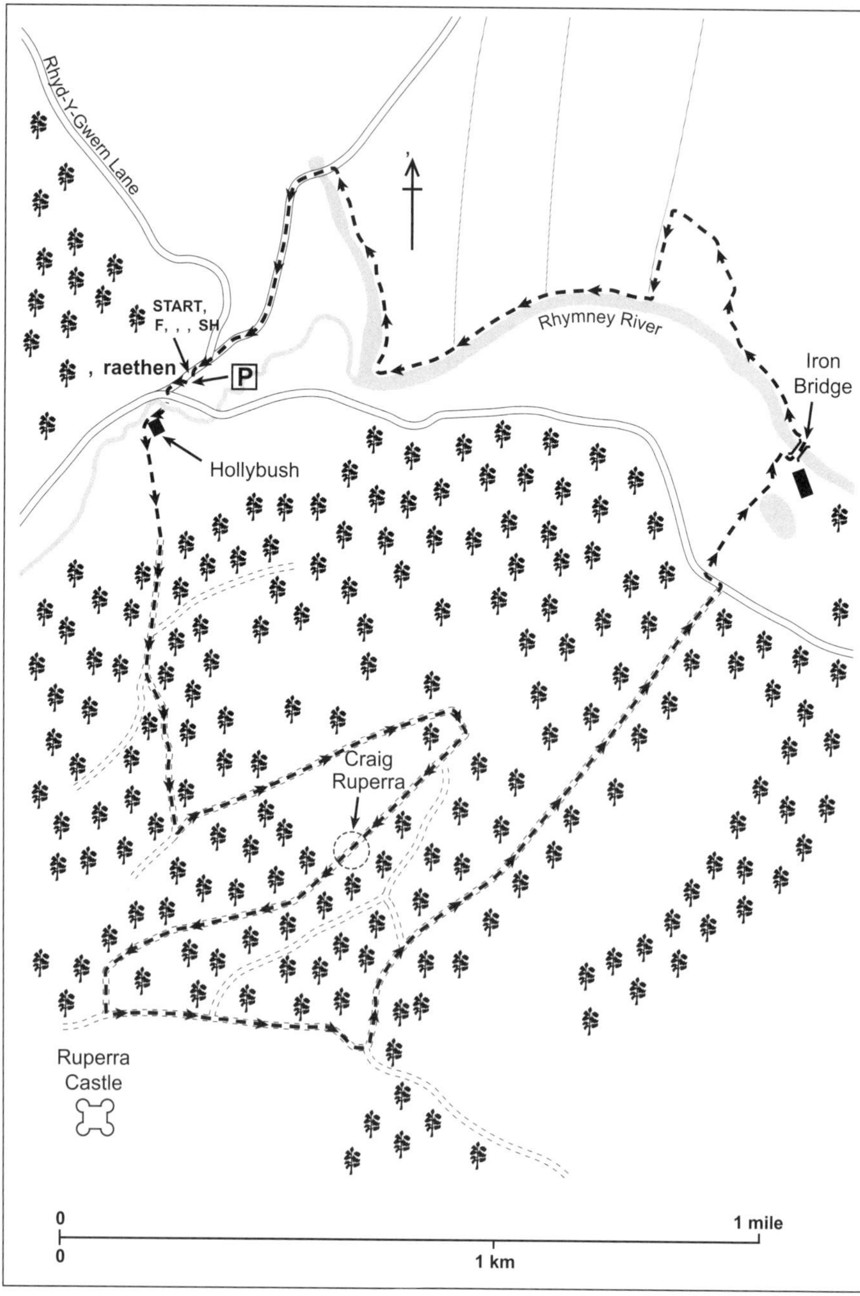
Rhyd-Y-Gwern Lane
START,
F, , , SH
, raethen
P
Hollybush
Rhymney River
Iron
Bridge
Craig
Ruperra
Ruperra
Castle
0
1 mile
0
1 km

the relatively small stile (ours didn't!), in which case there's a short detour. Just return to the road and, with your back to the pub, turn right, following the lane for a short distance until you reach the first entrance into the woods. This uphill track brings you back to the same woodland junction reached from the footpath behind the pub.

At the junction, two paths continue uphill in a fork. Take the left of these two, which is the slightly narrower path and quickly becomes extremely steep. Continue for a distance until the next junction and take the path bearing left. Things level out a little here and through the trees you can glimpse the landmark shape of Caerphilly Mountain. Then the path bends right and, as it rounds the crest of the hill, the views open up beautifully, all the way to Newport and the Severn Estuary.

Follow the trail to the kissing gate next to a bench overlooking the estuary. Go through the gate and up the final strait to Craig Ruperra, where an Iron Age hill fort stood more than 2,000 years ago, commanding spectacular views in all directions. Take a look at the information board and try imagining what it would have been like to live here all those years ago. We think of hill forts as being defensive strongholds, but it would have been very lively here with the marketplace and festivals.

In medieval times a motte and bailey castle – a raised earthen mound within a wall – was built here, but the tower walls still standing today don't date back that far. The land was once owned by the Morgan family, who built Ruperra Castle and of whom we'll hear more later. The Morgans built a two-storey summerhouse on Craig Ruperra in about 1700 and, in the early 1900s, added a thatched summerhouse within these thick walls and came here to drink tea! Mysteriously, however, this ruin is also known locally as Cadwgan's Tower, although it's unclear who Cadwgan was.

At the 'crossroads' turn left, following the 'G' waymarker downhill to a flight of steps, which leads to a wide track behind Ruperra Castle. Follow the track left, alongside the castle wall, passing another entrance back into the woods. Soon the views open up towards the castle and the estuary beyond. The castle is a sad ruin today and walkers can't get any closer than this as it's not safe, but it was once home to one of the most powerful men in Wales.

Not quite the picnic spot we were hoping for!

Ruperra Castle was built in 1626 by Sir Thomas Morgan, who had been knighted by King James I. It looked impressive but was a 'mock' castle, and the walls were not thick enough to be defensive. James' son, Charles I, stayed at Ruperra whilst gathering support in south Wales in the 1640s – although this was only a few years before he was beheaded for treason! The Royal coat of arms was added to the castle to commemorate his visit and the path from the nearby village of Rudry is still known as the King's Drive today.

Over the next 200 years, the Morgans – who also owned Tredegar House in Newport and all the land in between – added to the castle and rebuilt it after it was destroyed by fire. They also built an iron bridge, which we'll cross later in the trail, to take their carriage across the park and to church in Lower Machen. Godfrey Charles Morgan, Viscount Tredegar, took part in the famous Charge of the Light Brigade in 1854 and a statue of him on his horse, Sir Briggs, can be seen in Cardiff, outside the City Hall.

Like so many castles and stately homes, however, Ruperra was becoming too expensive to keep by the 1930s and was put up for sale, but there were no buyers. It was used briefly by the army during World War II but, despite later being bought by a developer, it's gradually fallen further into ruin. One tower has collapsed and huge cracks have appeared in the others, and it seems unlikely it will be restored to the grand house it used to be.

Continue along the track until reaching a clearing with metal gates and a wide track leading back into the woods. Follow this track all the way through the woods to the car park (the alternative starting point) and the road beyond. As you approach the road, a sparkling duck pond and a grand white house can be seen between the trees - and we're going to walk through the garden!

Strictly speaking, the public right of way runs along the right hand perimeter of the property and passes the duck pond in front of the house. However, the owners have put up a polite notice asking walkers to instead continue a few hundred yards along the road, to the left as you emerge from Coed Craig Ruperra, and take the steps down the left hand side of the lawn. As you draw level with the duck pond, the path veers left, into a field, and then quickly right, where you should be able to hear the sound of rushing water.

Follow the path to the banks of the Rhymney River where, to the rear of the large house, is the Iron Bridge. A few years ago it was becoming unsafe but a joint project by Caerphilly and Newport councils has restored it to its pre-Victorian best and it's now an important right of way between the local authorities again.

Cross the bridge and follow the path left to the metal gate and into a field. From here the track becomes a little less visible but the waymarkers help. Walk across the open field in the direction of the village of Lower Machen but, at waymarker 'O', turn left, away from the village and back towards the river.

The path continues upriver, over a small wooden bridge and around the curve of the river to the country road leading back to the

Draethen. At the road, turn left towards the village, taking care as you cross the extremely narrow bridge as it's a tight squeeze for traffic and there is no pavement.

On the restored Iron Bridge

WALK 11

On top of Old Smokey

Llanwonno, Pontypridd

Old Smokey is one of the iconic landmarks of the Rhondda Valleys and is so distinct it can be seen all the way from a viewpoint in the Fairytale Trail in walk 13, almost 15 miles away! It's actually called Tylerstown Tip and is an old coalmining 'spoil' tip that's now gone back to nature, but is known locally as Old Smokey as it resembles the flat peak of a volcano!

This is a refreshing walk if you want to get away from it all, mainly along level tracks but with one short but very steep scramble to reach the top of the spoil tip. The views are spectacular but they're not the only reason to visit! Young athletics fans gripped by Olympic fever might also want to give this trail a try – if you think Usain Bolt is impressive, here's the tale of a legendary Welsh runner called Guto Nyth Bran, who made history 250 years before Bolt was born! Throw in a filming location for 'Dr Who' and everyone in the family should be happy.

Approx. distance	**2 miles**
Approx. time	**1 hour**
Starting point	**Forestry car park, Llanwonno Grid ref: ST 0310 9570**
Grading	**An easy, mainly level walk with one short, steep scramble!**
Suggested age	**4+**
Maps	**OS Explorer 166; OS Landranger 170**

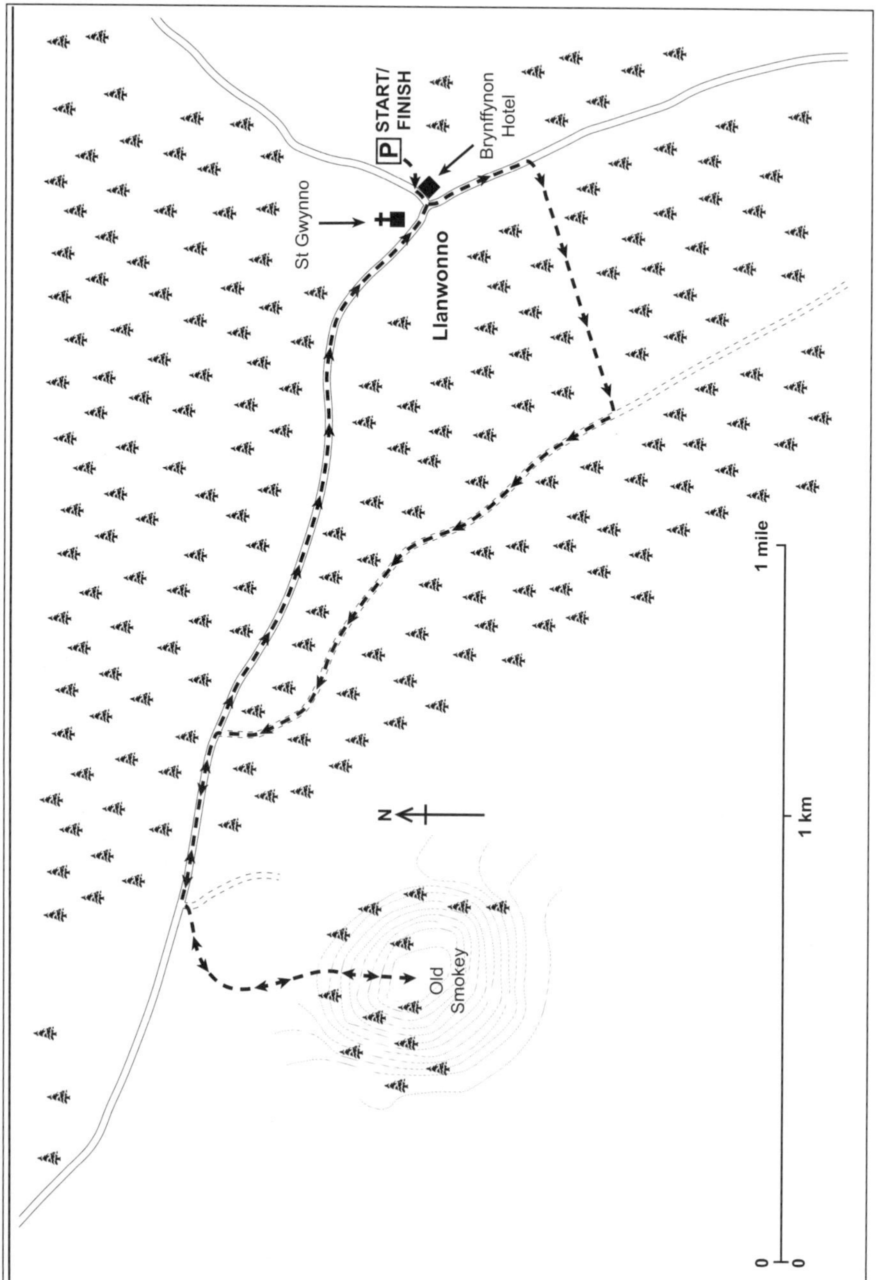
START/
FINISH
P
Brynffynon
Hotel
St Gwynno
Llanwonno
N
Old
Smokey
1 mile
1 km
0
0

The walk starts from a tiny place called Llanwonno, high on the mountain above Pontypridd. There are no houses, just a pub and the church of St Gwynno, but, despite this, it's a well-known place. The Brynffynon Hotel is renowned for its food, whilst the beautiful St Gwynno Forest contains a criss-cross of walking trails as well as the Celtic Trail cycling route 47, making it popular with cyclists.

The Llanwonno forestry is nature's playground!

From the forestry car park, turn left onto the road and walk uphill – carefully, as there's no pavement – to the Brynffynon Hotel. Turn left at the T-junction and follow the lane, enjoying the views across the valley. After several hundred yards, look for the yellow waymarked path on the right, leading into the forestry. It's a firm good, solid path to start with, although in poor weather it quickly becomes a little boggy so wellies are a good option. This trail makes a really good winter's walk on a crisp, snowy day, with the fir trees creating an enchanting Christmassy scene!

Where the footpath meets a wide forestry track, follow the track right in the direction of Old Smokey, which can be glimpsed through the trees. The path rises gently and there are lovely views below of St Gwynno Forest. It's incredibly peaceful up here most of the time – but be warned that there's a bike track in the valley and sometimes the peace is shattered by the noise of the engines!

Reaching the top of the rise, the track bends right towards a green and white metal gate in front of the mountain road. Turn left and walk for a short distance to the cattle grid on the brow of the hill. Just past the grid is a gap in the fence, from which you can cross the wasteland in front of the tip and start the scramble upwards!

From the top are far-reaching views of Rhondda Fach, the smaller of the two Rhondda Valleys. Below are the villages of Tylerstown and Stanleytown, whilst on the hill opposite is Penrhys and its enormous white shrine to the Virgin Mary. Religious people called pilgrims came

Running towards 'Old Smokey'

to Penrhys from all over Wales and beyond, and a well-trodden pilgrim trail called the Cistercian Way passed very close to Old Smokey. An original, smaller statue stood at Penrhys centuries ago, but it was taken to London in the turbulent Tudor times and burned!

From the top of Old Smokey, on a clear day you can also see the south Wales coast and, in the opposite direction, the Brecon Beacons. When you have enjoyed the views and had a good rest, climb back down to the road and cross the cattle grid. You can return along the forestry track or simply follow the mountain road back to Llanwonno, which is about half a mile away, and the church of St Gwynno.

Pop into the churchyard and take a look around. The oldest grave here dates back to 1667 but your challenge is to find the grave of Guto Nyth Bran, a superfast runner who allegedly could outrace a horse! Having won huge amounts of money from his races, Guto retired, but his girlfriend Sian persuaded him to run one last race, from Newport to Bedwas, against a new runner called the Prince of Bedwas.

The event took place in 1737, with Guto running the 12 miles in 53 minutes to win. That's the equivalent of running each mile in less than five minutes! To congratulate him, Sian clapped him on the back – but unfortunately this caused Guto to collapse and die on the spot!

To remember Guto and mark his astonishing achievements, a five-kilometre road race called Nos Galan is held in nearby Mountain Ash every New Year's Eve. You might not think that a fun run in the dark on a cold winter's evening sounds like a good idea, but it's been an incredibly popular event for more than half a century. Every year it's started by a famous 'mystery' runner, with sportspeople such as Wales and British Lions rugby star Shane Williams, cyclist Nicole Cooke and sprinter Linford Christie all taking part.

Did you find Guto's grave? We'll give you a clue – Guto Nyth Bran was only a nickname, after his parents' farm, which was called Nyth Bran. His real name was Griffith Morgan – good luck searching!

Legendary runner Guto Nyth Bran is buried here

You might also want to visit Llanwonno if you're a *Dr Who* fan and fancy walking around in Matt Smith's footsteps. Does the churchyard look strangely familiar? If so, it's probably because it was used as the location for an episode called *The Hungry Earth*, which was filmed here in 2009.

From St Gwynno's it's a short walk back to the car park, where there are several picnic tables and plenty more footpaths heading into the forest should you want to do some more exploring. The Brynffynon pub serves excellent food but its reputation means it is incredibly busy and you do need to book in advance.

WALK 12

Sunday Stroll

Church Village, Pontypridd

It's time to confess to a spot of bias with this trail! It's on our doorstep and is one of our favourite Sunday strolls when we just want to step out of our back door and go, leaving the car parked on the drive. That said, it's well worth visiting from further afield. It follows a section of the Church Village Community Route, which is a nice example of how road planners nowadays have to consider the surroundings and save as much wildlife and natural habitat as they possibly can.

Approx. distance	**2½ miles**
Approx. time	**1½ hours**
Starting point	**Station Road-A473 junction, Church Village, Pontypridd** **Grid ref: ST 0897 8523**
Grading	**An easy, mainly level walk along tarmac**
Suggested age	**All ages; pushchair friendly**
Maps	**OS Explorer 166; OS Landranger 170**

The walk starts from the roundabout at the junction of Station Road and the A473, where there is a small layby with room for several parked cars. Cross Station Road carefully and join the tarmac community route, with a small wood to the left and the bypass on your right.

The bypass runs from Cross Inn near Llantrisant to Power Station Hill in Tonteg. It was opened in 2010 but had been in the planning for 40

The Church Village Community Route opened in 2010

years before that! Local people had been campaigning since the late 1960s for a bypass to reduce the number of cars driving through their villages, especially as more and more homes were built in the area.

When the road finally did go ahead, however, it wasn't designed with just residents in mind! If today you travelled along the bypass by car from the Llantrisant direction to reach the start of the walk, you might have noticed some peculiar net tunnels suspended high above the road. These are dormice crossings! Dormice live in trees and can only cross safely *above* the road, not through the underpasses, so three crossings were put up to help them on their way. Also created were a number of ponds for the newts, frogs and slow worms that had made their homes in the area long before the bypass came along.

In September 2010 a community walk was held to celebrate the opening of the new road, with thousands of people taking over the tarmac for a day and walking four miles before it opened to traffic.

Now walkers and joggers can use this pleasant, green route instead, where the noise from the traffic is not as noticeable as you might expect due to the banks of shrubs and trees in between.

A little under half a mile along the community route, you'll arrive at a tall blue signpost. This was a Victorian cast iron vent originally used to ventilate sewers! For many years it was out of use and covered in ivy at the top of Power Station Hill, but it was restored, moved here and transformed into a local landmark with the help of children at a nearby school.

The artwork is inspired by Rhondda artist Ernst Zobole, who became well-known in the 20th century for his paintings of the south Wales valleys. The local schoolchildren studied his work and then copied Zobole's style to produce their ideas for sustainable and future transport. We think they did a brilliant job! The sign shows that this community route is part of a network of cycle paths running all the way from Fishguard in Pembrokeshire to Greenwich in London. The

It's a long way to Moscow from here!

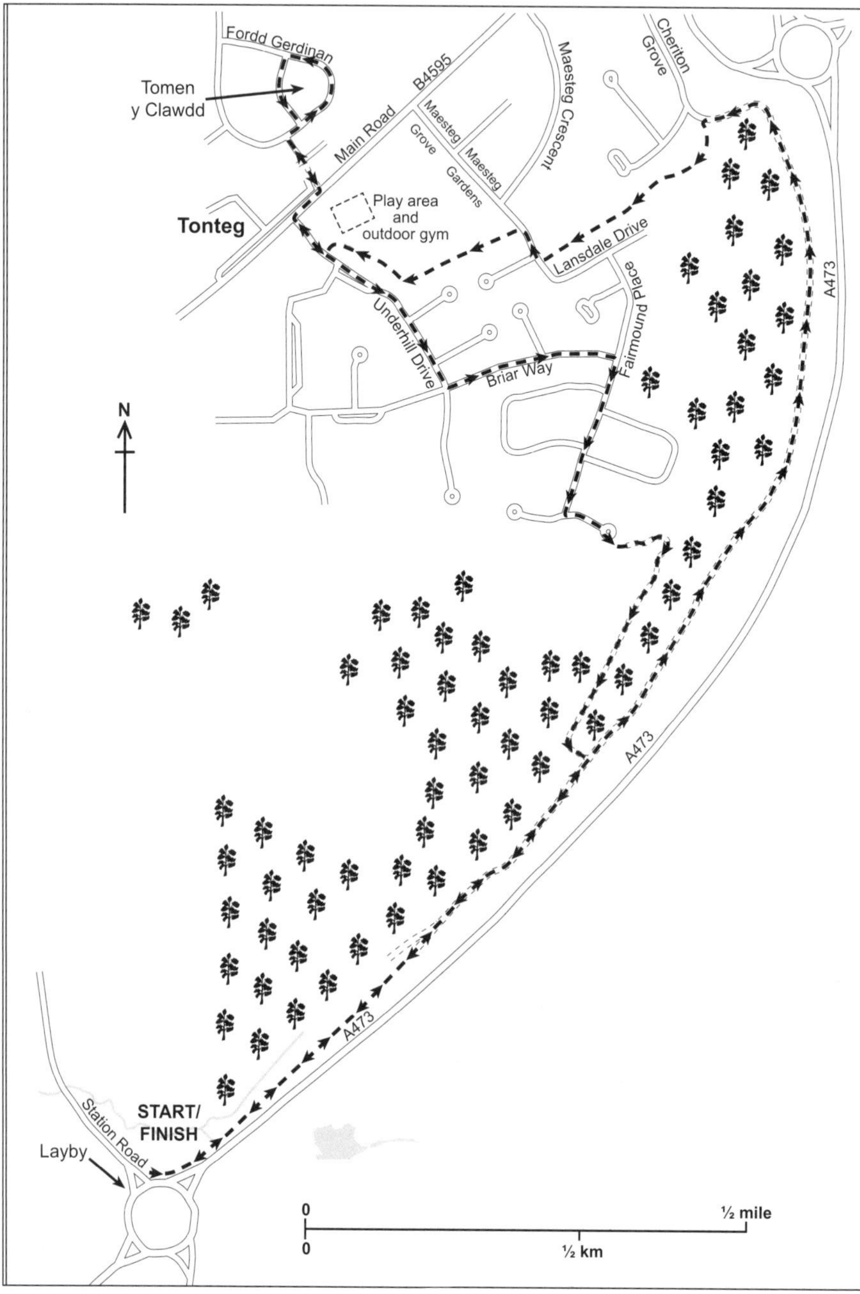
Fordd Gerdinan
Tomen
y Clawdd
Main Road
B4595
Maesteg Crescent
Cheriton
Grove
Maesteg
Grove
Maesteg
Gardens
Play area
and
outdoor gym
Tonteg
Lansdale Drive
Fairmound Place
Underhill Drive
Briar Way
A473
N
A473
A473
START/
FINISH
Station Road
Layby
0
½ mile
0
½ km

sign points to some other places too – can you name the countries Galway and Moscow are in?

A few hundred yards further on from the signpost is a clearing with picnic tables. Here there are also some white lines painted onto the tarmac, 100m apart, so you can have a quick race or two if you have enough energy!

Follow the community route for another half mile, where it comes to an end. This spot used to be Tonteg Junction, an extremely busy railway junction for transporting coal, although it's far more peaceful here now! Before the coalmines opened and thousands of people came to work in south Wales, Tonteg was a tiny place, with just two houses at a crossroads and a large mound where a medieval castle once stood. We'll find out more about it later on!

Go through the bicycle gate into Cheriton Grove and take the narrow tarmac footpath to the left, following it uphill past the back gardens of a number of houses. At the road, turn right past the bollards and then immediately follow the footpath on the other side of the road, running alongside the high fence. This grassy stretch runs past the playing fields to Tonteg play area, and an open-air fitness centre!

The outdoor gym equipment was installed quite recently and is good fun to try out. Also here are picnic tables, an outdoor ping-pong table and a playground, where just within the fence is a sturdy tree with a handy rope attached to help you climb it.

From the play area, continue up Underhill Drive to Main Road and cross at the lights a few steps to the right. Straight ahead is a short lane; follow this away from Main Road and turn right into Ffordd Gerdinan. There are houses only on one side, as in the middle of the crescent is a large mound. It doesn't look too impressive but it used to be very important!

This is the site of Tomen y Clawdd, a 'motte and bailey' castle built by the Normans who came from France to invade Britain almost a

Testing our fitness at the outdoor gym

thousand years ago. The castle was built to stop Welsh people attacking the Normans and had a moat around it to keep them out! It's now known locally as the 'Monkey Twmp' and until quite recently children were able to play on the mound, but this isn't allowed anymore as the site is so old and needs to be protected.

Walk all the way around Tomen y Clawdd, turning into West Mound Crescent to return to the lane. Retrace your steps back to Underhill Drive and follow it downhill, past the park, to the T-junction, where the trail turns left and uphill along Briar Way. At the brow of the hill, turn right and walk down Fairmound Place, taking the third street on the left as Fairmound Place branches in two. This leads into a quiet cul-de-sac, where a footpath leads out of the estate. Follow the footpath for approximately a quarter of a mile until it brings you back to the community route and the picnic area, where you can turn right and return to the start.

WALK 13

The Fairytale Trail

Castell Coch, Cardiff

This is a magical walk, starting and finishing at a fairytale castle built by a man who was said to be the richest in the world, and following an enchanting sculpture trail deep within the forest. Along the way are a number of dens and there's always the chance to make your own, of course, with all that the forest has to offer!

Looking for bears in Fforest Fawr

Fforest Fawr means 'Great Forest' and, although it's not actually that big, it offers a real getaway from the hustle and bustle of Cardiff just a mile or two away. It sits on the mountain between Cardiff and Caerphilly and has many paths and tracks for mountain bikers and walkers, including a section of the Taff Trail. On Caerphilly Mountain are a couple of pubs popular for their excellent food, as well as plenty of other attractions for families, so it's well worth making time for a full day of exploring and adventure.

Approx. distance	**1½ miles**
Approx. time	**1½ hours**
Starting point	**Castell Coch, Cardiff Grid ref: ST 1315 8279**
Grading	**An easy walk with one steep climb; possible for pushchairs but tricky in parts**
Suggested age	**4+**
Maps	**OS Explorer 166; OS Landranger 170**

The walk starts from Castell Coch, where there is a large free car park. Facing the castle, look for the information board at the edge of the trees on the right and follow the path into the forest. A number of trails start from here, including the one-mile Burges Way, waymarked in yellow, and Sir Henry's Trail, which is marked in red and almost two and a half miles long. Sir Henry Sidney was a courtier to Henry VIII and had an early ironworks in Tongwynlais, the village below Castell Coch.

Our trail follows National Cycle Network 8 and starts steeply alongside a wooden railing. It's a tough haul but it doesn't last long, soon reaching a T-junction where things level out. Continue ahead on the wide track through the forest, looking out for the log shelters built amongst the trees by the children who have been here before you. Feel free to pop inside for a rest!

Forest Fawr is managed by Natural Resources Wales and has been used as a film location many times. It was a busy industrial area for hundreds of years, with miners using dynamite to get to the iron ore from deep underground, but now it's wonderfully peaceful and scenic, especially in the spring when the ground disappears under a carpet of bluebells.

The path continues to climb through the forest, but more gently than the first section. After about half a mile from Castell Coch, on the left hand side, is the Three Bears Cave. Two bears stand guard near the entrance but we couldn't see the third! Creep past the bears, if you dare, to see the 'caves' – the arched entrances to three old mines. You can't go into them for safety reasons – and we don't think we'd go in even if we were allowed!

Return to the track and keep going uphill, where you very shortly arrive at a huge wooden arch leading into the Lost or Found Sculpture Trail. It was created by the Cardiff Outdoor Learning Wales group, who were asked by the Welsh Government to come up with an exciting trail to help children with their learning in the great outdoors.

The carved wooden sculptures are all clues to a giant creature that lives in the forest. You won't catch a glimpse of him but it's up to you to use your imagination, make up a story about the creature and share your tale! The clues to look out for include:

Bubble, bubble, there's lots of toil and trouble on this trail!

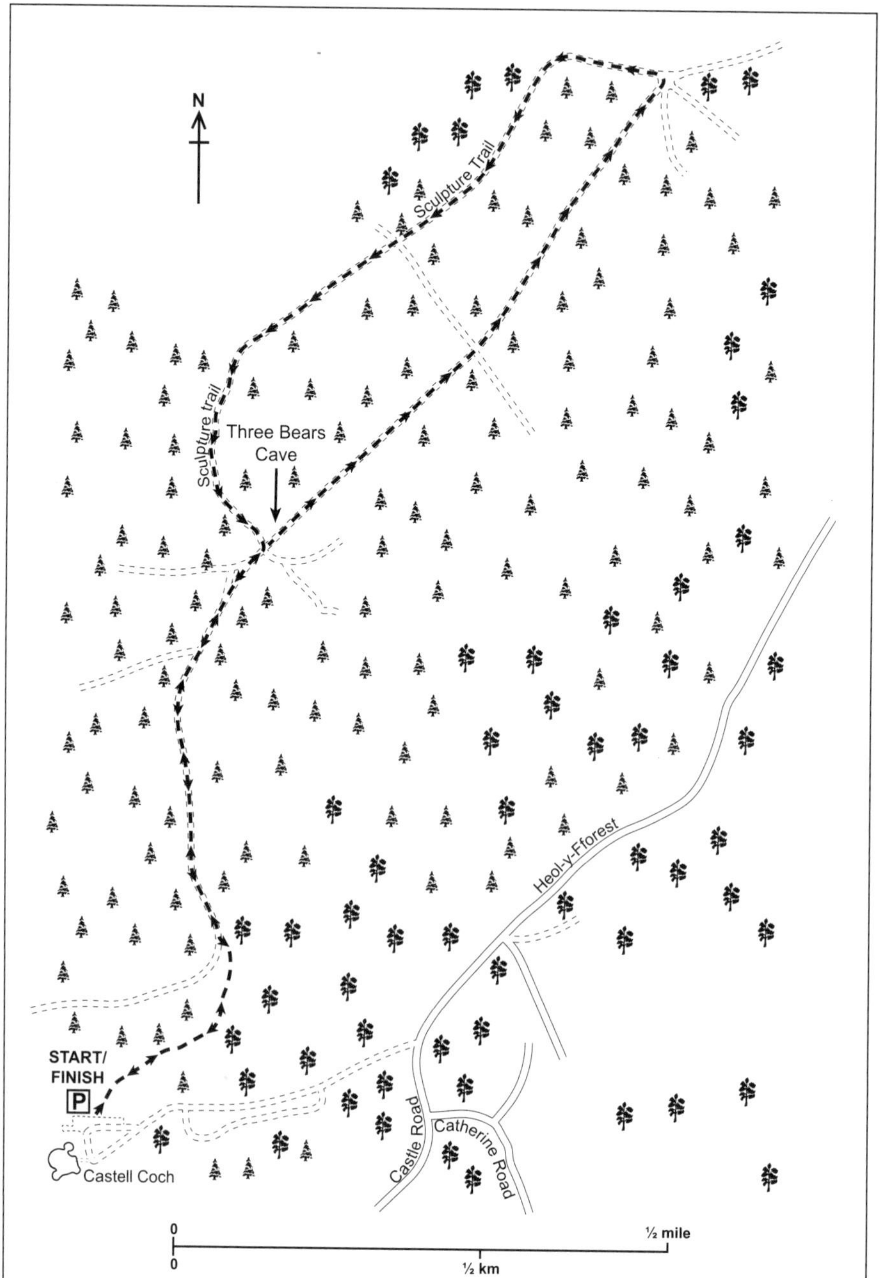
N
Sculpture Trail
Sculpture trail
Three Bears
Cave
Heol-y-Fforest
START/
FINISH
P
Castell Coch
Castle Road
Catherine Road
0
½ mile
0
½ km

A wizard
A watch
A cauldron
A dragon
A treasure chest
A chair

Be careful when you find the dragon, as something grisly is sticking out of his mouth... something you might use to run away quickly! Can you find the title of the book? And who is hiding in the moneybag nearby?

Behind the big chair (perfect for sitting on to tell your story) is a fun rope swing, whilst ahead is a vantage point to take in the lovely views up the valley. On a clear day, you can see all way to a very distinctive flat-topped mountain, miles into the distance, which you might recognise from Walk 11!

When you've completed the Lost or Found trail, return to the main track either via the entrance arch or by taking a short cut by the cauldron. At the fork in front of the cauldron (coming from the direction of the dragon), turn right and take the slightly uphill path. This brings you back to the Three Bears Cave, where you can turn right, along the main track, and walk back to the car park. Near the end, as the track curves around, look out for the path on the left returning down the steep section – it's easy to miss if you're too busy talking!

Making time for a visit to Castell Coch before or after your walk is highly recommended. Now in the care of Cadw, there is an admission charge but it's not expensive and well worth it. Visitors from all over the world know it as the 'fairytale' castle, and it does indeed look like a scene from a Hans Christian Andersen book!

It was dreamt up by the third Marquess of Bute, who had already created a fantasy home at Cardiff Castle at the end of the Victorian era with his vast riches. He had incredible amounts of money, partly

Cardiff's 'Fairytale Castle' *Photo used with kind permission of Cadw*

because he owned Cardiff Docks, which was the busiest port in the world, and also because he married a very wealthy wife! He found a friend in an architect called William Burges, whose imagination was as vivid as the Marquess', and together they came up with the idea of this Gothic getaway peeping out of the forest.

Castell Coch, which means 'Red Castle', has got everything - a drawbridge and portcullis, conical, turreted towers and a multitude of passageways and winding staircases to explore. The paintings, wall hangings and marble decoration in the rooms are dazzling, showing just how much money the Bute family had. But, despite the cost of building the castle, they never lived here and didn't even visit very often!

Today the castle is one of Cardiff's most famous landmarks, enjoyed by many visitors and also a magical venue for weddings. If this is your first visit, be warned that it probably won't be your last, as children tend to want to come back... and back... and back again!

WALK 14

Island Adventure

Flat Holm, Cardiff

This is a trail with a big difference - you need a boat to arrive! This fascinating walk probably won't take as long as the boat trip to get here, yet there's an enormous amount to see and learn and you'll certainly get plenty of fresh air!

Flat Holm is tiny in size - less than half a mile wide - but its significance is huge, both in terms of the wildlife it shelters, including slow worms and one of the largest gull colonies in Wales, and historically. In 1897, an Italian inventor called Guglielmo Marconi sent the world's first wireless message across water from Flat Holm! We might not listen to the radio very much nowadays but, without his experiment, we wouldn't have much of the technology we rely on today. The message travelled nearly four miles to Lavernock Point near Penarth and simply said: Are you ready? So, with that in mind... are you?

A number of operators run trips to the island on scheduled days, one a pleasure cruise service from Weston Super Mare and Cardiff Bay and

Approx. distance	**1 mile**
Approx. time	**3 hours (factoring in round trip)**
Starting point	**The jetty, Flat Holm Island, Bristol Channel Grid ref: ST 2208 6489**
Grading	**A gentle stroll around grassy island paths**
Suggested age	**Suitable for all ages; not pushchair friendly**
Maps	**OS Explorer 151; OS Landranger 171**

another an exhilarating rib expedition from Cardiff Bay. The former is the gentler way to travel and gives about six hours on the island, perfect for bird watching and soaking up the peace.

Speed junkies will love the ribs, powered speedboats which, in comparison, give only two hours on Flat Holm but are a thrilling way to get there! Please do note, however, that the ribs are no good for families with small children as passengers must be at least 1.2m tall. Also, they are not for the faint-hearted, as the water can be extremely choppy and the waves huge. You WILL get wet, so take waterproofs and just enjoy the ride!

Flat Holm's lighthouse runs on solar power today!

Other things to remember before you plan your trip include the fact that all voyages are weather dependent and bookings can be cancelled at frustratingly short notice for safety reasons. And a cheap day out this is not; the boat fare for a family of four costs about £100 and there's also an island landing fee of £5 for adults and £2.50 for

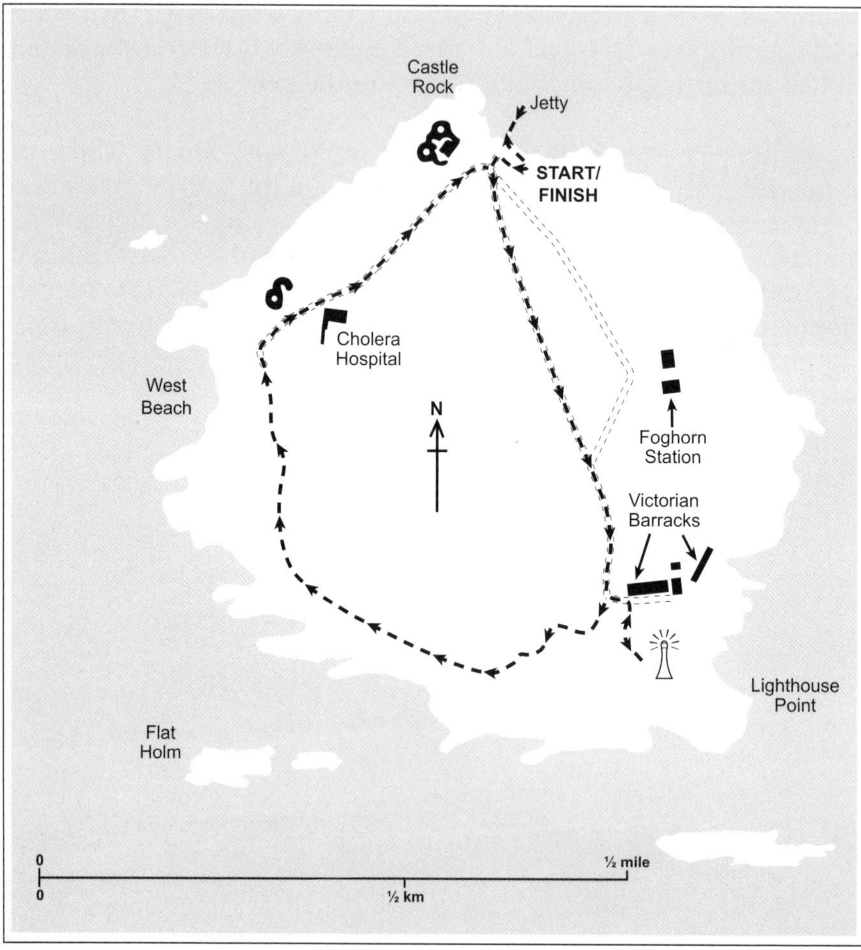

children. But the expense and potential delays are incredibly worthwhile; visiting Flat Holm is a privilege and gives families the chance to do something genuinely out of the ordinary.

The adventure starts before you even land on Flat Holm, when the boat navigates the Cardiff Bay Barrage. Once Cardiff was the busiest port in the world, with cargo ships sailing all over the globe from the Oval Basin and the Coal Exchange. By the end of the 20th century the area was extremely run down, but the barrage has transformed the old Cardiff Docks into one of Wales' most popular attractions for families and visitors.

Three enormous locks allow vessels to leave the calm waters of Cardiff Bay and it can be quite daunting sitting in the shadow of the eight-metre high lock gates, waiting to head into the blustery Severn Estuary! When the lock gates are closed, the barrage bridge allows pedestrians to cross from one side to another, enabling walkers to complete a four-mile circular walk right around the bay. And the technology isn't just to benefit tourists and sailors! The barrage has one of the most advanced fish passes in Europe, giving salmon and sea trout a safe route to Cardiff's rivers, recorded by special underwater cameras.

After flying over enormous waves, the rib makes a complete circle of Flat Holm to showcase the views before mooring at East Beach. At the jetty, visitors are greeted by warden Stewart Grey and a number of volunteers, who stay on the island to carry out research and help maintain the land. From here, the group is guided along the 'main' track to the Victorian barracks, where a brief history of the island is outlined and where you can leave belongings whilst you head off to explore.

Although today the warden is the only permanent resident, Flat Holm has been occupied for more than 800 years and used as a retreat for almost twice as long as that! The first person known to have come here was St Cadoc, who founded a monastery in Llantwit Major 1,500 years ago and frequently visited Flat Holm to seek peace and quiet. Later, in 918, Danish Vikings hid out on the island after being defeated by the Saxon army and, in fact, 'holm' is the Danish word for 'river island'.

The discovery of bits of medieval pottery shows that people lived here from the end of the 12th century and it's thought that a large building - possibly a chapel - stood here a little later. Flat Holm has been part of the Cardiff parish of St Mary since Glamorganshire was formed just after the Battle of Hastings in 1066, and services have continued to be held on the island until fairly recently.

The Victorian barracks were built to house 50 soldiers manning Flat Holm's four batteries, although in fact only a master gunner and five gunners were stationed here. Today the barracks are used as an education centre and include a tiny museum crammed with fascinating clues to island life. A small but very well stocked shop is also open on visitor days and there's another room that the grown-ups will appreciate – a pub, the most southerly in Wales and possibly the smallest! At the bar, snacks such as crisps and nuts are available but no hot food is served.

In front of the barracks is the lighthouse, which was built in 1737 following a tragedy a year earlier, when 60 soldiers drowned near Flat Holm. To start with, the light was powered by coal carried by the keepers from the store all the way to the top of the tower – and they got through 25 tons every month! Almost 100 years later, a new oil-burning lamp replaced the original, coal-fired one and remained in use until 1969, when the light was converted to run on electricity. Today, the lighthouse runs on solar power and can be seen more than 20 miles away!

From the lighthouse you can see Steep Holm, another previously fortified island which is now a privately owned nature reserve and which you can also visit. Facing Steep Holm from the lighthouse is the spot to see some of Flat Holm's famous wild leeks, which, when in flower, have pretty purple heads and can grow up to six feet tall! The leeks grow only in five locations in the UK and you aren't allowed to pick them.

Also in front of the lighthouse is a large concrete hole; this is one of the gun pits built in case of an invasion by the French army! The Victorians were terrified of this happening and built a series of forts and defences all along the south coast. The work cost the equivalent of millions of pounds – but the invasion never came!

Flat Holm and Steep Holm were heavily fortified and these pits contained huge guns, which could be raised to fire out to sea and then lowered and hidden again. An early photographer came to the island

Neighbouring Steep Holm island, behind Flat Holm's giant leeks!

in 1875 and persuaded a gunner to raise the gun into its firing position so he could photograph it with the lighthouse in the background, but this caused the gunner to get into big trouble!

From the gun pit, follow the island perimeter clockwise, away from the cluster of buildings. Depending on the time of year of your visit, signs might warn you away from certain paths, where gulls make their nests. An incredible 4,000 pairs of lesser black backed gulls nest on the island's plateau, whilst 300 pairs of herring gulls nest on the rocks and cliffs. The gulls are self-sustaining, laying more or fewer eggs as needed. You don't have to look too closely to spot baby gulls hopping along the paths and in the grass but look out, as those flying overhead have been known to target visitors with their mess!

Walk around the island towards West Beach, passing the concrete remains of a Second World War command post on the way. The outbreak of the war dramatically changed life on Flat Holm, as Cardiff was heavily bombed during the Blitz and the Bristol Channel islands were needed to defend the coastline. Two batteries – the north and south – were built and 350 soldiers stationed on the island. If the siren sounded to warn of enemy aircraft, the batteries had to be manned – by 150 soldiers each – in three minutes!

From West Beach, take a look at the unusual wave cut limestone plane, which formed about 300 million years ago! There are a number of caves on this side and the north side of the island, and it's believed that 18th century smugglers used them, and a series of natural tunnels, to store forbidden goods, including tea and brandy!

At West Beach the chimneys of a derelict building come into view. This was the isolation hospital, designed to stop outbreaks of cholera reaching the mainland. Cholera is a horrible bacterial disease caused by drinking dirty water or eating contaminated food and which, in Victorian times, killed thousands of people. The hospital originally

The island is a birdwatcher's paradise

consisted of tents and housed three cholera-stricken sailors, one of whom died. There were complaints about the hospital from other island occupants, including the troops stationed there, the lighthouse keepers and the farmers, whose vegetables and rabbits could no longer be sold at Cardiff market in case of contamination.

Following a couple of serious cholera outbreaks and many patients coming to the island, it was decided that a new hospital should be built and it opened in 1896. But, by then, cholera was already starting to wane, so patients with yellow fever and even the plague were also sent there!

A short walk from the hospital ruins is a whitewashed farmhouse that was once the Flat Holm Hotel. A skittle alley was built alongside the walled garden and business thrived due to the number of day-trippers visiting from Cardiff and Barry, although eventually the parish's strict licensing hours – rather than the tide times – led to a decline in trade and the hotel closed in the 1930s.

Continue walking clockwise around the island to return to the north side, where there are impressive views of Castle Rock. Nearby is the jetty, but if you have time before your return boat journey, you can head back to the barracks, passing on your left the old Fog Horn Station, to find out more about the island's history and Marconi's pioneering work.

Marconi was just 22 when he arrived in Britain, stung by the lack of interest in his ideas in Italy. Having already sent a wireless message on Salisbury Plain, he came to Flat Holm with his assistant, a Cardiff Post Office engineer called George Kemp, to see if messages could be transmitted across water. A pair of masts over 100ft tall was assembled on the island and on the mainland and, on 13 May 1897, the world's first overseas message, sent by Morse Code, reached Lavernock Point.

Just days later, another message was sent nine miles from Lavernock to Brean Down and, by the end of 1901, Marconi and Kemp had transmitted a wireless signal across the Atlantic, from Cornwall to Canada – disproving those who thought it impossible as the curve of the earth would get in the way!

If you have time, head back to the area just east of the barracks, where you'll see a huge, sloping tiled construction. This is a water-catcher, designed to collect rainwater and store it in a deep underwater tank. It was originally built to supply soldiers based here and now stores water for the warden and volunteers.

For more than 30 years, the island has been managed by the Flat Holm Project, part of Cardiff Council, but this is due to change in 2016 with a new partnership involving the National Trust and the RSPB. After a time of uncertainty, Flat Holm again looks set to continue drawing wildlife and visitors to its shores for many years to come.

WALK 15

To the Lighthouse

Vale of Glamorgan

This scenic clifftop walk along the Glamorgan Heritage Coast enjoys spectacular views and plenty of sea air to blow away the cobwebs! Unsuitable for pushchairs, it's also not a walk for very young children as the rise and fall of the coast path can be quite challenging. For older children, however, it gives the chance to get up close to a working lighthouse, see a castle that looks straight out of a Hollywood film set and go off the beaten track in hidden woodland.

The Glamorgan Heritage Coast is a 14-mile section of coastline between Aberthaw and Porthcawl. The limestone cliffs are millions of years old and dinosaur fossils from the Jurassic age have been found further along the coast! Due to the nature of the cliffs, however, and the very real danger of falling rocks, it's essential to stick to the footpaths and keep a very close eye on children.

Approx. distance	**4½ miles**
Approx. time	**3 hours**
Starting point	**King George's Field, St Donats, the Vale of Glamorgan Grid ref: SS 9403 6821**
Grading	**A cliff top trail with several steep climbs**
Suggested age	**6+**
Maps	**OS Explorer 151; OS Landranger 170**

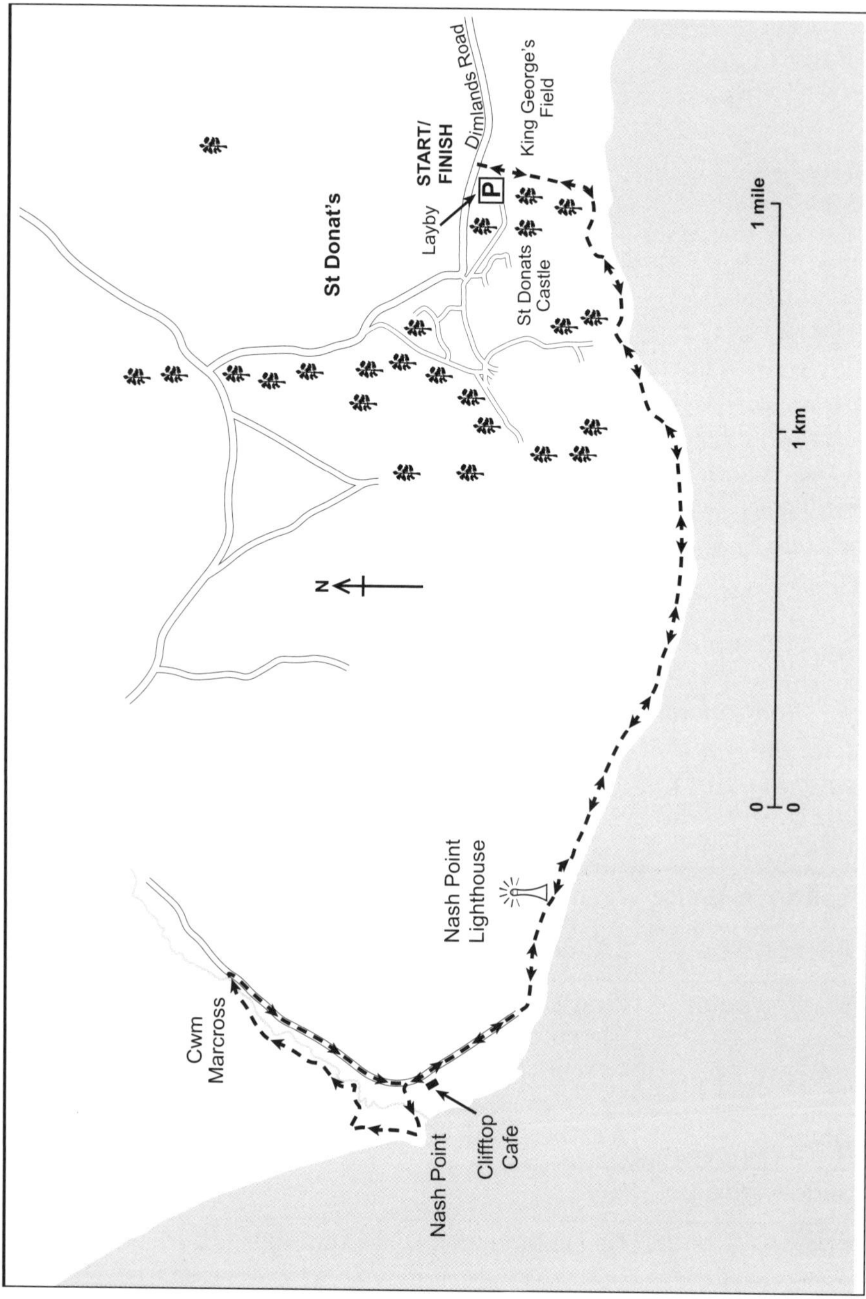
St Donat's
START/
FINISH
Dimlands Road
King George's
Field
Layby
P
St Donats
Castle
N
1 mile
1 km
0
0
Nash Point
Lighthouse
Cwm
Marcross
Nash Point
Clifftop
Cafe

The walk starts on the outskirts of St Donats, a tiny village known for its castle and church. The best place to park is in a layby at the entrance to King George's Field, alongside the castle grounds. From the layby go through the metal kissing gate - which is a surprisingly tight squeeze! - and follow the public footpath along the edge of the playing field towards the sea. Go through the wooden gate to follow the track and then turn right at the yellow and blue Wales Coast Path sign, through the kissing gate, before the track reaches the edge of the field.

Follow the woodland path alongside the castle grounds, keeping right at the fork (the left hand path leads directly to the beach) and looking out for the castle as it comes into view. Many castles in Wales are 'mock' versions, built by wealthy families to replicate earlier fortresses, but St Donats really was a castle, built 700 years ago. It's believed that an incredible 23 generations of the Stradling family owned it one after another!

St Donats Castle, now a college, overlooks the bay

Nash Point was the last manned lighthouse in Britain

In 1925 the castle was bought by a rich American newspaper owner and for the last 50 years it's been a renowned college, attracting students from all over the world. The coast path runs alongside the battlement wall and down to the slipway, where students often gather to sit in the sunshine and enjoy the view over St Donats Bay.

Reaching the far side of the slipway, take the stone steps back into the woods, continuing to follow the coast path signs. Take care in the woods as the path can be muddy, with uneven steps and a number of stiles to cross. Carry on through the woods until the path emerges and the first glimpse of Nash Point Lighthouse can be seen in the distance. The lighthouse is nearly 200 years old and was built using stone quarried from the cliffs below. It was the last lighthouse in the British Isles to be manned, switching to an automated light in 1998, and was operated by three keepers living in the neighbouring cottages.

Up close, the lighthouse is in gleaming condition and extremely impressive. If you time your visit well you can go inside, as the visitor centre is open during most weekends and bank holidays throughout spring and summer, as well as Wednesdays during school holidays. For safety, however, anyone wishing to climb the tower has to be at least 1.1m tall. From the lantern room are far-reaching views across the Bristol Channel to the north Devon coastline, as well as along the Heritage Coast and further west.

Today it's possible to get married inside the lighthouse and, in fact, a wedding was being held on the day we passed on our walk. Note, though, that the lighthouse isn't open to the public if a wedding or civil partnership is taking place. The smaller, flatter building next to the lighthouse is for the fog signal, which was in use for 90 years and is still sounded during weddings and school visits. The neat white and green cottages next along were the keepers' cottages, which are now hired out to holidaymakers.

Continue on the tarmac path along the Nash Point headland, reaching the Clifftop Café. It's small but Tardis-like, stocking tourism leaflets and local art as well as selling hot and cold snacks, and there are also toilets for customers. The information board outside tells the history of the coastline which, although beautiful, was a very dangerous spot before the lighthouse was built. Ships have been wrecked off these cliffs since Roman times and in 1831 a ship called *The Frolic* sank with no survivors, leading to the lighthouse being built. Marking the tragedy is a small plaque a few yards away from the tarmac path, just as the cliff starts to dip.

Enjoying a rest before the steep climb

Take the cliff path in front of the plaque down into Cwm Marcross. The cliff rises up again steeply on the other side and the next bit is optional! If you don't fancy the climb, turn away from the sea and follow the valley floor into the woods ahead. But if you want some more spectacular views, start climbing! We made the effort and thought the scene from the top was definitely worth it.

An Iron Age fort once stood on this headland, in an excellent position for spying approaching invaders. Follow the path away from the sea and then, as the path starts to veer left, look for the wide track heading back down into Cwm Marcross. At the bottom, pick up the thin path into the woods, which contrast sharply with the coastal section and are quite enchanting! As the path winds through the woods, a series of stepping-stones lead back and forth over the shallow, babbling stream. How many times do you cross the water?

Eventually the woodland path reaches a large gap in the mesh fence. Don't go through the gap but follow the steps on the right and cross the bridge, very carefully after wet weather, as the ground can be extremely slippery. Join the road and turn right, again taking care until you re-join the coast path, as there's no pavement. Soon Nash Point Lighthouse looms into view again and, from here, you can return to St Donats the way you came.

WALK 16

The Tinkinswood Trail

Dyffryn, Vale of Glamorgan

This is a gentle walk that's mainly on the level although, as the ground is often uneven, it's unsuitable for buggies. A section is along a country lane with no pavement, where it's essential to supervise children properly, but otherwise this lovely circular walk allows children to run through fields, see lots of nature and get up close to a huge and very interesting piece of prehistory!

The walk starts from Dyffryn Gardens, where parking is with the kind permission of the National Trust. The grounds are open from 10am to 6pm in summer and 10am to 4pm in winter, although it is best to check the Dyffryn Gardens page of the Trust website ahead of your visit, as these hours sometimes change slightly.

Approx. distance	**2½ miles**
Approx. time	**1½ hours**
Starting point	**Dyffryn Gardens, Vale of Glamorgan** **Grid ref: ST 0966 7260**
Grading	**An easy route through fields and along a country lane**
Suggested age	**5+**
Maps	**OS Explorer 151; OS Landranger 170**

From the car park, follow the drive back to the main gates and turn right onto Dyffryn Lane. Follow the lane for about half a mile and turn right at the T-junction, which leads to Dyffryn village. After the bend,

Making grass trumpets at Dyffryn; one of the National Trust's '50 things' to do

look for the red letterbox set into the wall and turn right over the small stone bridge next to Doghill Farm.

Immediately after the bridge, cross the stile into the field on the right and head to the top, looking out for the friendly horses and ponies who live here! At the top is another stile into a second field. Cross this field, passing the telegraph pole in the middle, and walk through the wide gate into a third field. Heading past the large tree in the middle of this field, walk to the hedge and go into field number four. Follow this field uphill, remembering to close the first two metal gates behind you to keep the animals in.

Go over the stile next to the third metal gate and walk towards the pylon at the top of the field. To here from Doghill Farm, you've been following the Millennium Heritage Trail, which is a 65-mile path right around the Vale of Glamorgan. Can you imagine walking the whole 65 miles? It might take more than one day! This footpath and hundreds

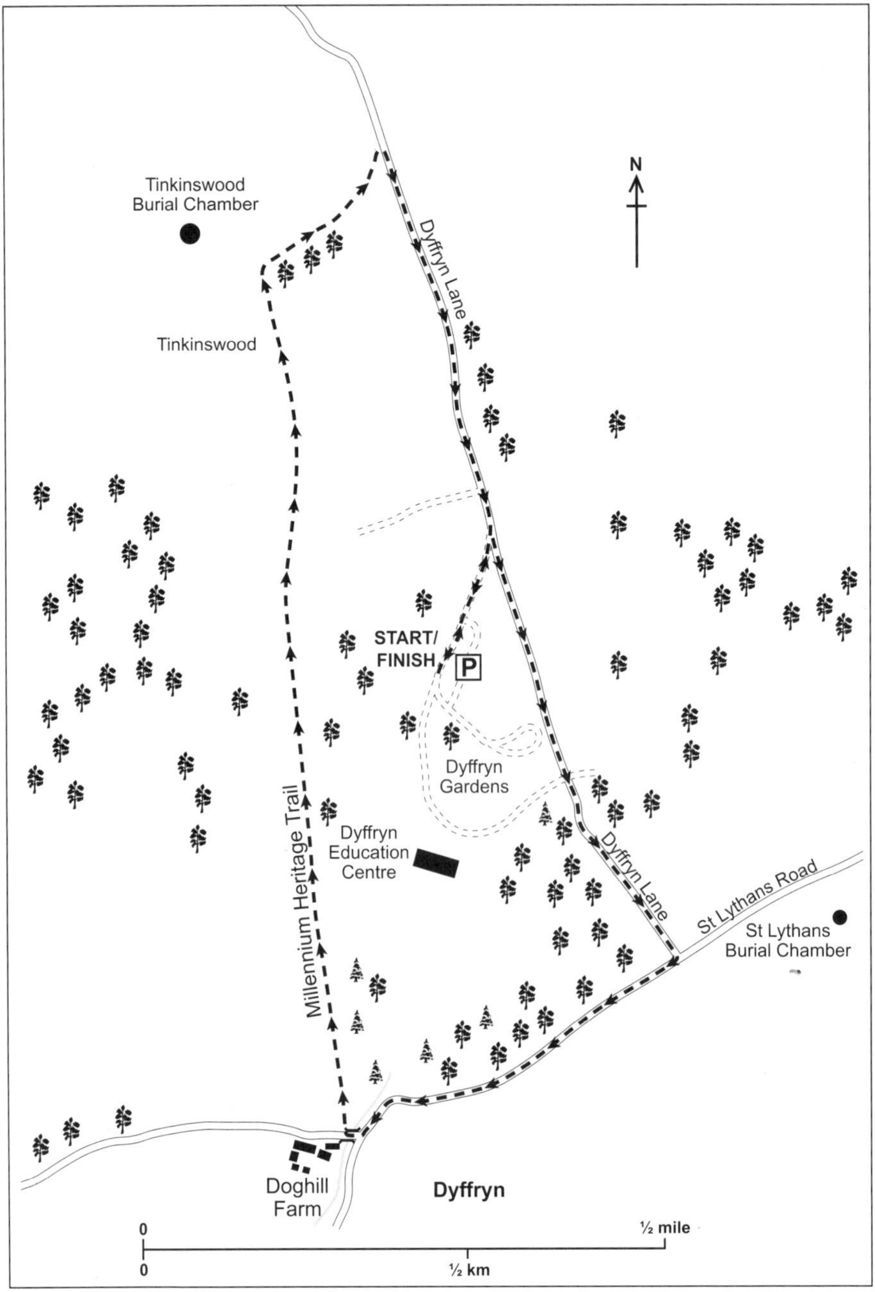

Tinkinswood
Burial Chamber
N
Dyffryn Lane
Tinkinswood
START/
FINISH
P
Dyffryn
Gardens
Dyffryn
Education
Centre
Millennium Heritage Trail
Dyffryn Lane
St Lythans Road
St Lythans
Burial Chamber
Doghill
Farm
Dyffryn
0
½ mile
0
½ km

of miles of paths in the Vale are looked after by a charity called Valeways, and you might see some of their volunteers cutting back hedges and overgrowth during your walk.

At the pylon, follow the path right and look out for Tinkinswood Burial Chamber – it's hard to miss! Just inside the kissing gate leading to the chamber is a wind-up listening post, where you can find out all about the tomb's history. Today it looks like a funny shelter made from huge stones, but 6,000 years ago it was a very important site for burying people and holding ceremonies.

There are many prehistoric chambers like this in Wales but Tinkinswood is one of the biggest. The enormous stone on the top, called the capstone, is thought to be the biggest in Britain and weighs as much as five double decker buses! The tomb was opened up a hundred years ago and the excavators found bones from about 50 people. They also discovered pieces of pottery, as well as belongings

Tinkinswood burial chamber is nearly 6,000 years old!

from the Bronze Age and Roman times, showing that the chamber was in use for many years.

Tinkinswood isn't the only prehistoric burial chamber near here. Think back to the T-junction leading to Dyffryn village. If you had walked left instead of right, you would have come to another tomb called St Lythans, which, like Tinkinswood, is cared for by Cadw and is also about 6,000 years old, although it's not quite as large. It was excavated in 2011 and is known as Gwal y Filiast, which is Welsh for 'the Greyhound's Kennel'.

Tinkinswood is a lovely place to be on a warm, sunny day but it's probably quite creepy here at night! Over the years, many stories about this site have sprung up and it's said that anyone who spends a night here at certain times of the year will die, go mad or become a poet! Do you think that's true?

From the chamber, return through the metal gate and walk straight ahead along the edge of the field, with the trees on your right. In these trees is a quarry, which is thought to be where the chamber's stones came from originally. How do you think the people who built the tomb moved the stones without diggers or cranes? In prehistoric times, stones were often rolled on logs to a new spot, and it's thought that it took 200 people to lift the Tinkinswood capstone into place!

It can be a bit of a trudge through long grass until the far end of the field but, once you're through the hedge, the path is clearer and easier going. Follow the path to a small layby and you're back at Dyffryn Lane. Turn right, again taking care when traffic passes. Along this lane are sycamore trees, which have seeds known as 'helicopters' due to their shape and the way they rotate through the air. If you see some on the ground, throw them into the air and watch them spin!

From here it's a short walk back to the main gates of Dyffryn Gardens. The grand mansion you see today was built as the family home of a man called John Cory; he built Barry docks and, as tons of Welsh coal set sail across the world from Barry, he was incredibly rich. But the estate passed out of the hands of the Cory family less than 50 years after it was bought and has since been used for all sorts of things, including a police academy and even a dog training centre!

The National Trust took the property over in 2013 and has started to transform the house, which was in a bad state of repair. It's very different to many Trust houses in that it was bought without a stick of original furniture and as a result each room has been designed and refurbished to be explored and played in – in other words, there are no 'do not touch' signs! Visitors can also learn more about John Cory and his children, including a son called Reginald who designed the gardens.

Looking for dragonflies at Dyffryn Gardens

The gardens are incredibly special – so much so, in fact, that Dyffryn was voted the most special place in Wales in 2015. This trail definitely doesn't stop at the house, with many more turns and hidden corners to continue exploring outdoors, although you can make up your own route from here! The grounds are divided up into a number of sections, each strikingly different from the last, such as the formal lawns, the beautiful beds of dahlias and the kitchen garden. Our favourite place, however, is the arboretum, with its winding paths and handy log benches. It's also a great place to have a go at grass trumpet blowing, which is one of the National Trust's '50 things to do before you're 11¾' (and is harder than it looks!)

Dyffryn also has a massive glasshouse with a collection of huge cacti, small ponds full of dragonfly and damselfly and a children's play area. And if it's too cold for a picnic pop into the tearoom, where delicious treats are made with ingredients grown in the garden, such as lavender and rose cakes and beetroot scones!

WALK 17

A Day in the Dunes

Kenfig

In fresh contrast to both the smoggy skyline of Port Talbot steelworks to the west and the neat promenade of seaside resort Porthcawl to the east are the wild and windswept sand dunes of Kenfig National Nature Reserve. With the cobalt water of Kenfig Pool sparkling at its core and with a rich habitat of birds and plants, this is a special place of secret hideaways and hidden histories, of rugged trails and tranquillity.

Although not a very long route, the effort of trekking through sand can make it seem longer than it actually is! Whilst many children will enjoy the opportunity to explore the dunes, families with young children might prefer to reach the bird hide, about three quarters of a mile from the start, and then turn back. Due to local authority budget cuts, sadly the reserve visitor centre is no longer open daily to the public, although it remains available for school and group bookings and visitors can use the toilets.

Approx. distance	**4 miles**
Approx. time	**2-3 hours**
Starting point	**Kenfig National Nature Reserve, Ton Kenfig, Bridgend** **Grid ref: SS 8013 8100**
Grading	**A trek through fields, dunes and sandy paths**
Suggested age	**5+**
Maps	**OS Explorer 151; OS Landranger 170**

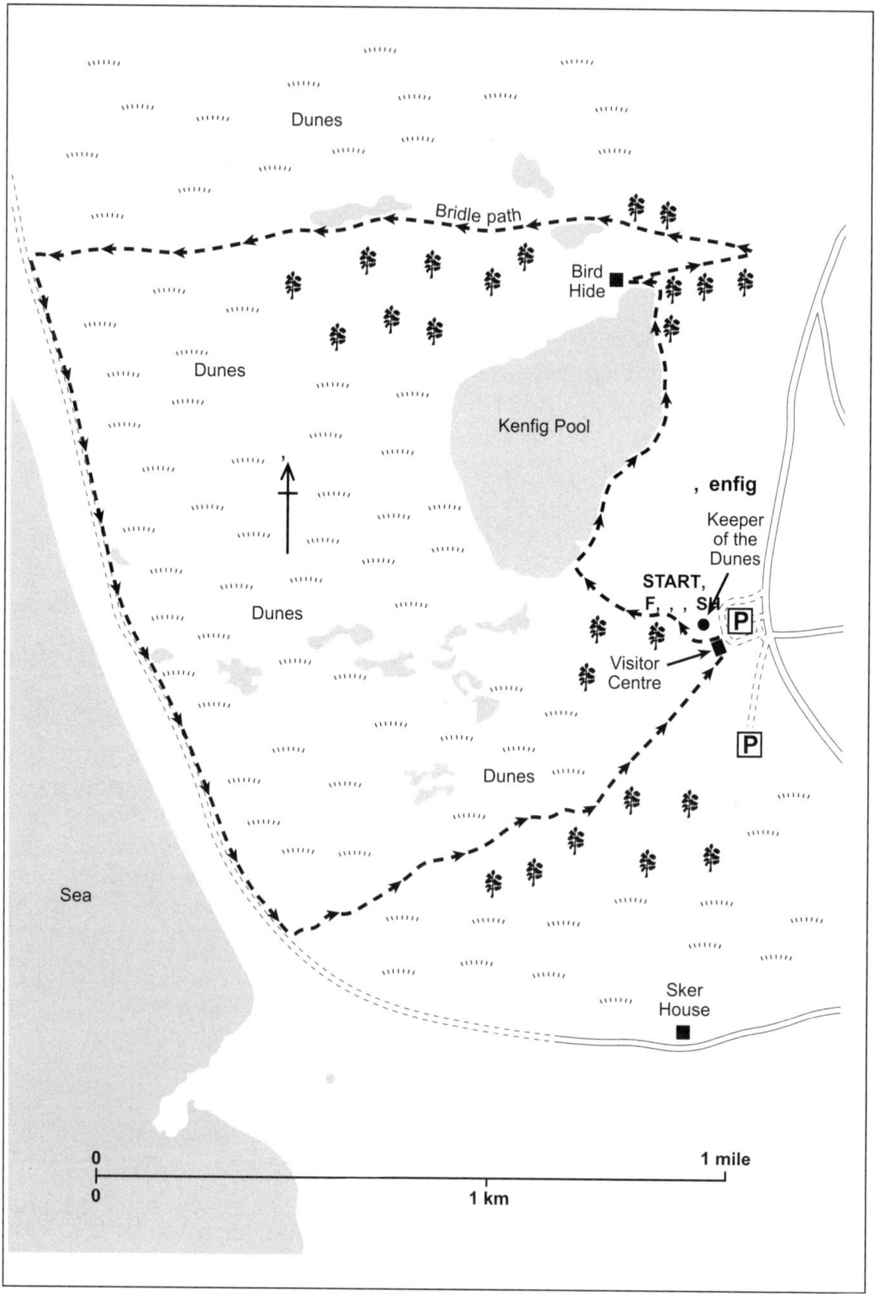

Dunes
Bridle path
Bird Hide
Dunes
Kenfig Pool
, enfig
Keeper of the Dunes
START,
F, , , SH
Dunes
Visitor Centre
P
P
Dunes
Sea
Sker House
0
1 mile
0
1 km

Park in the car park and start from the visitor centre building, next to which a stunning carved oak figure stands guard. This is the Keeper of the Dunes, one of an inventive series of 'Nature Keepers' sited throughout the Bridgend countryside, created to boost tourism. You can find out more about the keepers and how they came about in Walk 20, which contains a trail with a difference at Bryngarw Country Park! In the meantime, visitors can download to smartphones and tablets a special app called 'Dare to Discover', which will guide you to each keeper throughout the county. With this app, you can press the flame symbol on reaching the Keeper of the Dunes and listen to her story!

Stand next to the Keeper and look out across Kenfig Pool. It's hard to imagine, but one of the biggest towns in south Wales used to stand on this now sand-covered land! Kenfig was a thriving medieval walled town founded almost 1,000 years ago by a man called Robert, Earl of Gloucester. It had a castle and keep, a high street and a guildhall and

The Keeper of the Dunes guards the reserve

could make by-laws and raise its own taxes (a power not even held by the Welsh Government at the time of writing!).

But Kenfig was attacked by enemies many times and was burned down so often that the townspeople built a fence of logs around the perimeter, with sharp, pointy tops to keep raiders out. Unfortunately the fence was struck by lightning and burned down again! Then, in 1405, Kenfig was attacked and destroyed by Owain Glyndwr, the last native Welshman to be crowned Prince of Wales. The town was rebuilt yet again, but within 50 years it came under attack by a different invader - nature. The sand from the dunes crept inland, gradually engulfing the streets and forcing residents to abandon the town in favour of Pyle, further from the shore.

Today, all that remains of the town is the castle mound, visible in the dunes to the north of Kenfig Pool, an ancient church and the Prince of Wales inn, which was built in 1605 as a town hall to replace the one buried by sand. Local legend has it that the old town is buried deep beneath Kenfig Pool itself - but in fact the water is very shallow, with no trace of old buildings at the bottom at all!

Follow the tarmac path away from the visitor centre towards Kenfig Pool. At the vantage point, take the short flight of steps leading to the water's edge and, from the small, sandy 'beach', look for the narrow footpath following the shoreline anti-clockwise. Cross the wooden stile, taking care as the water can lap right up to it after heavy rain, and follow the path through a number of fields and over a series of stiles towards the trees on the far shore.

The path goes into the trees and to a small clearing, where a raised boardwalk leads to one of the pond's two bird hides. From here you can spot ducks, swans, and egrets, whilst if you're very lucky you might see a kingfisher or hear the cuckoo that has made his home at Kenfig recently.

From the bird hide, retrace your steps to the clearing and follow the gravel path slightly uphill. For a short distance you'll be walking away

Ducks on Kenfig Pool

from the pond, before meeting a bridleway and turning back in a 'V' shape just as a couple of houses come into view. The bridleway is marked by blue signs and is the start of a mile-long trek up and over the dunes.

On our soggy spring walk we found sections of the main bridleway to be flooded, but a tapestry of smaller footpaths runs through the dunes and you can pick out your own route quite easily. Although it's a while before the sea comes into view, you can probably already hear the distant swish of the waves and so should be able to keep heading in the right direction!

The dunes are nearly 4,000 years old and once stretched all the way from the Ogmore River to the Gower Peninsula, before a chain of villages and towns was built along the south Wales coast. Today the reserve is internationally known for its rare plants, whilst local people like to walk here armed with metal detectors!

Eventually the bridleway and footpaths meet a wide track running horizontally through the dunes in front of one final ridge. Climb the ridge and the stunning Sker Beach stretches ahead of you into the distance, rewardingly remote despite its three miles of golden sand because as it takes so long to get to!

After a picnic or a quick sandcastle contest, return to the wide track and head east. Soon you will notice a series of yellow waymarkers dotted along the left side of the track. At Sker Point, waymarker no.12 leads back into the dunes and to the nature reserve car park. However, if you like spooky stories, continue along the track a short distance until you spy a rooftop lined with distinctive chimneys in the distance. This is Sker House – 'Sker' by name and scary by nature!

A house has stood on this extremely isolated spot for 900 years. Originally a monastery farm, a grand house was later built around the Great Hall. In the 1700s, Sker House was owned by a man called Isaac Williams, and it's said he kept his daughter Elizabeth confined to one room to stop her marrying a local harpist called Thomas Evans. She eventually died of a broken heart and several people have claimed to see her ghost in an upstairs window, watching over the moors and waiting for Thomas to come!

Elizabeth was known as the 'Maid of Sker', although other female residents over the years have also claimed the title! The name has gone down in history, with *Lorna Doone* author RD Blackmore writing a book called *The Maid of Sker*, about a foundling washed up on the coast of Glamorganshire, whilst in Brisbane, Australia, a paddle steamer of the same name was built in the 1880s!

Sker House is now privately owned and under renovation, with no access through the grounds. But it's interesting to take a look and imagine it in the old days, with monks working in the fields and the old house creaking and groaning as the sharp sea winds howled all around.

Return to the waymarker and make your way along the wide path through the dunes. The track here is smoother than the earlier

Back through the dunes

bridleway, so it's easier on the legs and not far to the car park. From here are views inland to the sweeping landscape above Margam and the five landmark squares of woodland on the hillside.

The trail soon runs alongside a golf course, so watch out for balls whizzing by! Several narrower paths lead into the dunes at various points, but keep to the main track to get back to the start.

WALK 18

Sand and Castles

Merthyr Mawr, Bridgend

It's best to wear your wellies for this one, as there's a good chance your toes will get wet! This trail takes you from Ogmore Castle to the enormous sand dunes in Merthyr Mawr National Nature Reserve… via a series of stepping-stones that takes a little nerve to cross! Then there's the challenge of the 'Big Dipper', an enormous bank of sand that's tiring to haul yourself up but well worth the effort – if only for the pleasure of launching yourself back down!

Due to the stepping-stones and the nature of the dunes, the walk as described is unsuitable for buggies and wheelchairs. An alternative from Ogmore Castle is to follow the road upriver for a third of a mile and cross at the bridge on the official Wales Coast Path route. It's then possible to reach Candleston Castle and return without climbing the dunes, although there is still a country road to navigate and this might not be considered ideal for families with pushchairs.

Approx. distance	**3½ miles**
Approx. time	**2 hours**
Starting point	**Ogmore Castle, B4524, Vale of Glamorgan Grid ref: SS 8819 7694**
Grading	**A mainly level walk with one big climb**
Suggested age	**5+**
Maps	**OS Explorer 151; OS Landranger 170**

This walk is in the heart of the Glamorgan Heritage Coast, a stunning 28-mile stretch of Wales spanning Bridgend and the Vale of Glamorgan.

It starts at Ogmore Castle, about a mile inland from the sea. The castle sits on the banks of the River Ewenny, one of many built along the Welsh coast by the Norman invaders. There's a small riverside car park just below the castle, which can fill up quickly on weekends and school holidays and is where the walk starts.

The first section is the trickiest – crossing the stepping-stones! It's probably best not to try to count them in case you lose concentration and fall in the water, but there are said to be 52 altogether. According to local legend, a girl living in the castle fell in love with a handsome man who lived on the other side of the river, so they built the steps as a way of being able to visit each other. There are plenty more legends surrounding this trail, so read on!

At low tide, it's easy and enjoyable for young children to walk across the stones, although adults might opt to wade through the water alongside them, holding their hands just in case! Even in winter, the crossing remains more than manageable in good weather, but if the

Crossing the stepping-stones

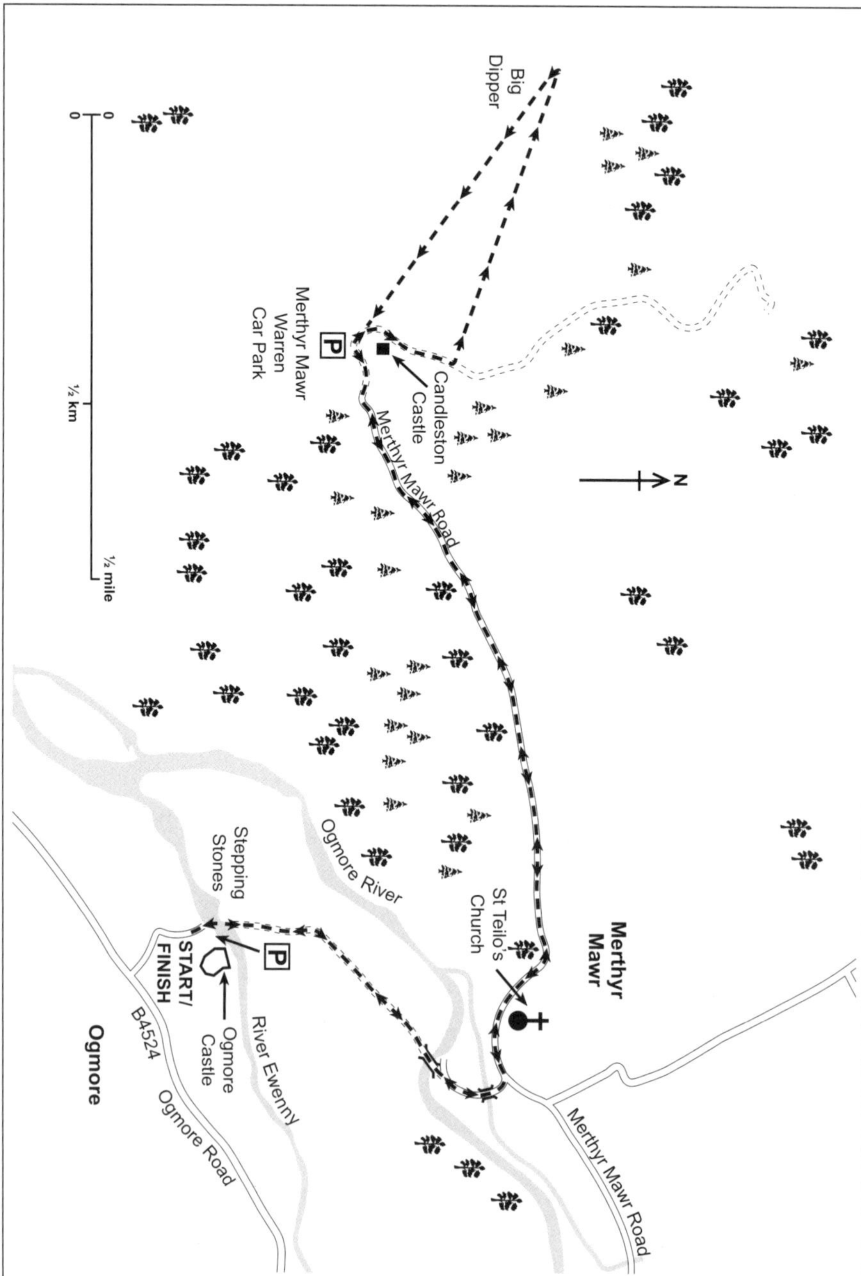
Big Dipper
Merthyr Mawr Warren Car Park
Candleston Castle
Merthyr Mawr Road
N
0
0
½ km
½ mile
Merthyr Mawr
St Teilo's Church
Ogmore River
Stepping Stones
START/ FINISH
Ogmore Castle
River Ewenny
B4524
Ogmore
Ogmore Road
Merthyr Mawr Road

stones are slippery or the river is particularly fast moving, it's up to each family to decide if it's the right thing for them. Whatever the time of year, do check the tide times ahead of your walk, as plenty of people have been stranded on the wrong side by rising water!

Once across the stepping-stones, follow the path ahead to the white footbridge visible in the distance. Legend has it that this 'V'-shaped parcel of land in between the rivers Ewenny and Ogmore was where King Arthur fought his last battle. Fatally wounded, his body was hidden in a cave in nearby Coed y Mwstwr Forest as his troops thought that news of his death would divide the kingdom. It would be nice to think this story is true... but there are so many locations in Wales said to be connected to King Arthur it can be hard to know which to believe!

Cross the Ogmore River at the bridge, which is known locally as the 'swing bridge' or the 'swinging bridge' because an earlier version built here in the 1840s was notorious for swaying from side to side! Have no fear about crossing the current bridge, however, as it's a later replacement that is very secure!

The trail now joins the Bridgend Coast Path, an eleven and a half-mile section of the Wales Coast Path running all the way to Kenfig National Nature Reserve, which features in Walk 17. Follow the path as it curves around to the tiny village of Merthyr Mawr, made up of pretty thatched cottages, and turn left along Merthyrmawr Road.

There's no pavement from here to the dunes so take extra care; it's usually a quiet lane but it can be busier in the summer when more traffic is heading to the dunes. The Highway Code advises walkers to keep on the right hand side, where they can see oncoming traffic, and walk in single file when needed. Large groups of people should walk on the left, again in single file or in pairs.

Follow the road for about a mile, passing St Teilo's Church, more cottages and a cluster of artists' studios. It leads to Merthyr Mawr Warren car park, where there are public toilets if needed. In the trees just to the right is Candleston Castle, another ruin, although not quite as old as Ogmore Castle.

The castle was built as a fortified manor house in the 1400s by a rich family called the de Cantaloupes, from whose name 'Candleston' is thought to have come. The castle is said to be haunted, and its lonely position in the woods can certainly seem a little creepy! This is where the mysterious tale of a lost village comes in. It's believed that Candleston once stood very close to a place called Treganlaw, Welsh for 'the town of a hundred hands'. What happened to the houses and the people isn't exactly known, although it's thought that, as at Kenfig, the land was gradually buried over many years by sand blowing in from the dunes and the residents had to flee. The castle continued to be occupied until the middle of the 19th century, when it was abandoned and eventually became this ivy-covered ruin.

With Candleston Castle on your right, follow the track straight ahead into the wood. Very soon there's a small path bearing left from the

The ruins of Candleston Castle

main track and a small wooden footbridge crossing the stream. In front, the 'Big Dipper' rises up, its sand a striking orange. Now for the hard part – the leg-wobbling tough climb to the top!

This is the highest sand dune system in Wales and one of the highest in Europe, with fantastic views back towards Ogmore Castle and an aerial view of Candleston in the trees below. Many people think that the dunes look like the Sahara Desert in Africa, the largest hot desert in the world, and some scenes from the famous movie *Lawrence of Arabia* were filmed here in the 1960s. Archaeologists have found artefacts such as Stone Age flints, Bronze Age pottery and Roman tiles showing that people have lived in this area for thousands of years, and in the last century a dig revealed a small Roman settlement called Burrows Well, which disappeared into the dunes long before the shifting sands reached Candleston.

The dunes are an important place for nature and are home to many species of bird and insect, as well as some rare flowers and plants. It's a fabulous place to explore, with many trails running in all directions from the Big Dipper to the other dunes and across the 'slacks', the flat areas in between. The dunes are often busy and you might see people sledging down the slopes, even in the summer when there's no snow! It's important, however, to play safely and never tunnel into the dunes, as this could cause the sand to collapse.

From here and with a good map you can extend your walk to Newton or even further to the picturesque village of Tythegston. Otherwise, head back down the dunes towards Candleston and make the return journey back to Ogmore Castle.

In the whitewashed cottage next to the castle is a lovely tearoom, whilst over the road the Pelican pub is known for its food. And if you have time, travel the extra mile along the road to the beautiful sands at Ogmore-by-Sea, one of Bridgend's most popular places no matter what the weather or the time of year – in fact, it can be especially busy on Christmas Day!

WALK 19

Calon Lan Clamber

Garw Valley, Bridgend

This is a challenging walk with a steep scramble up and down the mountainside. For energetic children, it's an adventurous trail in exciting forestry, with lots of interesting species to see and great spaces to explore. But be prepared for some muddy sections, as well as the possibility of overgrown paths the deeper into the forest you go!

This is hearty Welsh countryside and, although the tarmac path circling the pretty lake at Parc Calon Lan is accessible for everyone, it's a different story the higher you climb. Suitable footwear and warm clothing are essential and I'd also recommend carrying snacks and drinks. In return for your efforts, you'll be spoilt for choice for picnic spots with birds-eye views of the peaceful Garw Valley.

Approx. distance	**3 miles**
Approx. time	**2 hours**
Starting point	**Parc Calon Lan, Blaengarw, Bridgend** **Grid ref: SS 8997 9301**
Grading	**Very steep and challenging in places**
Suggested age	**6+**
Maps	**OS Explorer 166; OS Landranger 170**

The trail begins and ends at Parc Calon Lan, a pretty lakeside park in Blaengarw at the head of the valley. If you're Welsh or if you like rugby, there's a good chance you know a very famous hymn called

Calon Lan. The words were written more than 100 years ago by a Welsh poet called Daniel James. He grew up in Swansea but later moved with his wife and five children to Herbert Street in Blaengarw, where he is thought to have written the hymn. As well as remaining popular in churches and chapels, it's usually sung by fans when Wales plays at the Millennium Stadium in Cardiff!

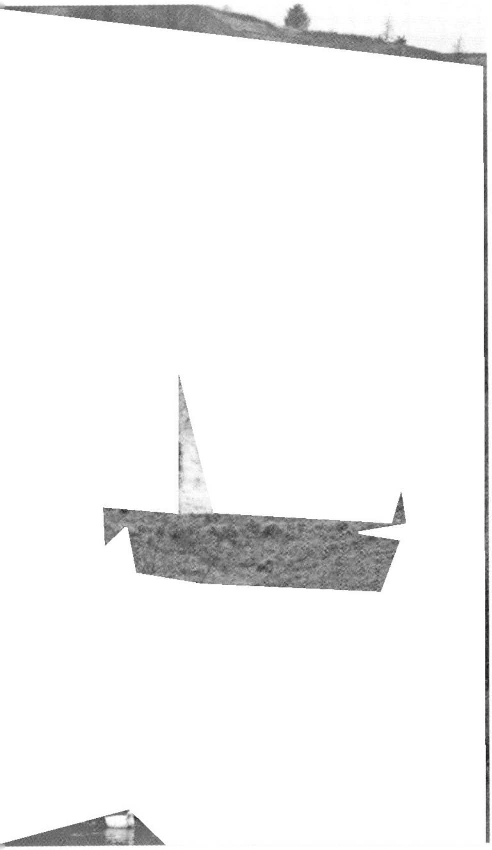

In the heart of the Garw Valley

In Daniel's time, the area in which the park now stands was a coal 'washery'. This was the place where the coal from the local mines was separated from mud and ash and the dirty water would be washed away into the river. No wonder the Afon Garw used to be called the Afon Du, or the Black River! Luckily, it is now much cleaner and home to birds including dippers, grey wagtails and grey herons and fish.

In 2008, long after the mines had closed, the area was in need of regeneration, so the local community obtained funding and created Parc Calon Lan. It was opened by BBC news presenter Huw Edwards and is now the starting point of a series of stimulating mountain trails. Although it's a pretty and popular spot, however, families should note there are few facilities; there's no café and the tiny visitor centre and toilets aren't always open.

The trail starts at the visitor car park just off Railway Terrace. With your back to the visitor centre and facing the lake, follow the tarmac

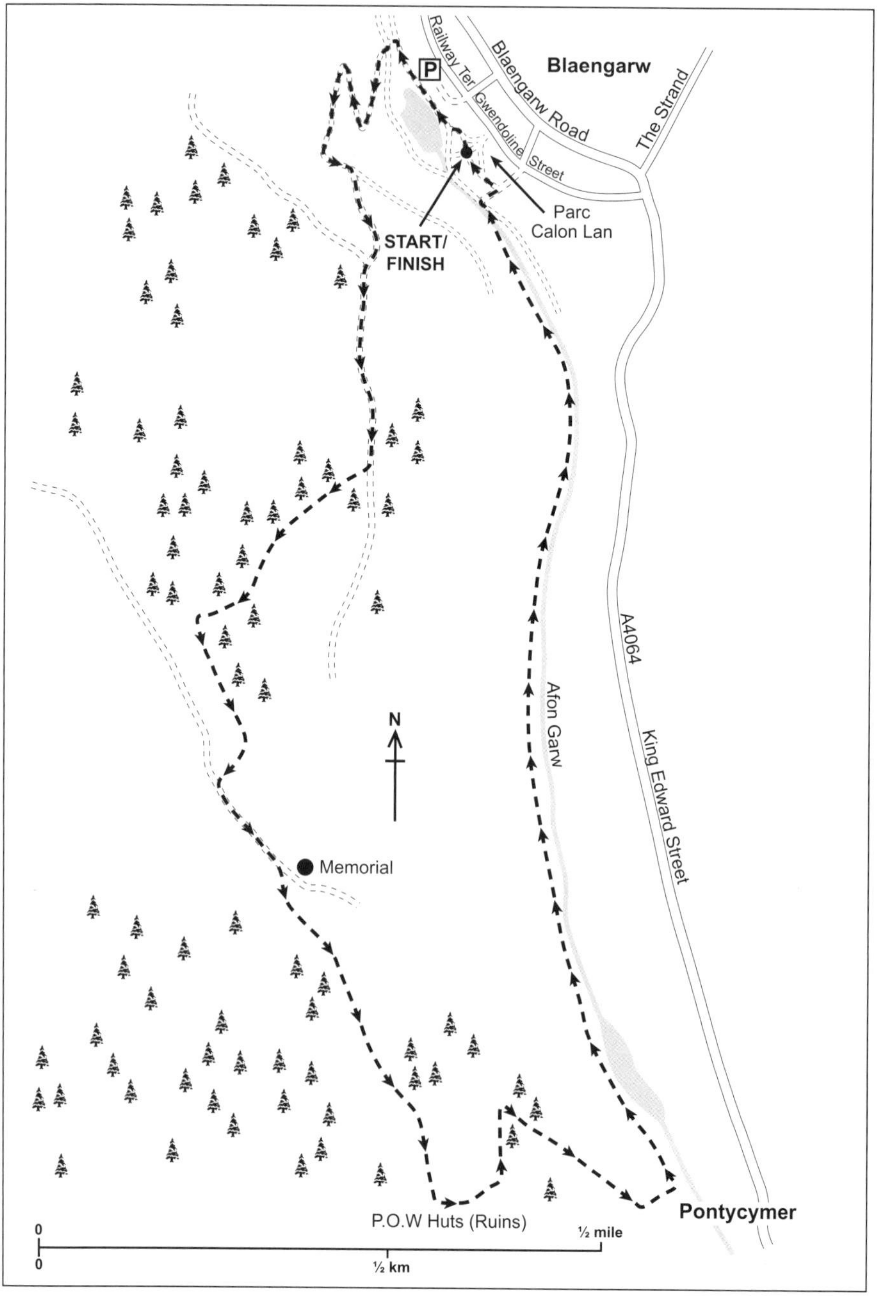

Railway Ter
Blaengarw Road
Blaengarw
The Strand
Gwendoline
Street
Parc
Calon Lan
START/
FINISH
P
A4064
Afon Garw
King Edward Street
N
Memorial
P.O.W Huts (Ruins)
Pontycymer
0
½ mile
0
½ km

path anti-clockwise, circling the top of the lake. At this point you are briefly following a blue waymarked mountain biking trail, which takes you over a small wooden bridge. Don't follow the community route but walk straight ahead on the gravel path, which starts climbing upwards. At the small bench the path zigzags back and forth and there are lovely views from here over Parc Calon Lan and the Garw Valley, as well as an orchard of native trees such as apple, ash and birch trees planted by school children and local volunteers.

It's getting a little steep now – and it's about to get steeper! Go over a second wooden bridge crossing a small culvert and follow the signs marking the path on the right, uphill and through a round metal gate with a stile next to it. You're now entering Darren Fawr Woods, which has tall conifer trees such as Scots pine and spruce. If you're lucky you might see birds like woodpeckers or wood warblers, and there are also lots of butterflies in the summer.

After a sharp climb of about 100m, the path forks. Ignore the blue waymarkers pointing left, as they lead back to the community route and the lake. Instead, follow the wide track signposted with black waymarkers. After a very steep section the path gets a bit thinner as it flattens out slightly, then it climbs steeply again and becomes little more than a narrow footpath (one of the sections which can get quite muddy!). It's quite hard going at this point, but we're nearly at the top!

The woods are a popular area for mountain biking, with two Darren Fawr trails starting at Parc Calon Lan. The blue Glengarw trail is for intermediate bikers and the black Gellideg track is for those with more experience. It's really important to read the signs in this area as some paths are for walkers and bikers whilst others are for bikers only, and you could get hurt on the wrong route.

About three quarters of a mile from the car park, the footpath merges with a wider track, again clearly marked by white signs warning of bikes approaching from the right. Follow the track left into the Scots pine woodland until the trees clear and the landscape levels out. It's bikes only to the right, so keep to the left, along the grassy path.

The views get better the higher you climb

Soon after leaving the woods, look for the Welsh national flag down the hill and to the left, which is a memorial to a local soldier who was killed in Iraq in 2007. Walk down towards the flagpole and bench, taking extra care if it's muddy as the hillside is steep. It's a lovely spot for picnics, with fantastic views of the valley, and it's popular with walkers using the alternative track coming up directly from the community route below. If the climb to this point has proved enough for little legs, this track offers a good 'escape' route; just walk straight down and turn left onto the tarmac path back to Parc Calon Lan.

For those completing the full trail, however, take a few steps down the scree from the flag and hop across the culvert at its shallowest point. Climb back up to the ridge and head left on the trail, now better defined again. There are more great views from here – see if you can spot the blue house amongst the terraces below!

The trail goes back into the forest again. Carry on for about half a mile, until the trees start to clear and a track drops sharply downhill to the left. This is the way we need to go but, first, walk a short distance to the right and look for some ruined stone walls. These are said to be huts lived in by German prisoners during the Second World War, which ended 70 years ago. The prisoners were kept here during the war and planted many of the trees in the forest today.

When you're ready, follow the steep path downhill, taking care on the loose stones. At the first waymarker, turn right on a narrow path. From here it looks to simply drop off the side of the mountain but, as you follow it, it just narrows and continues downhill. At the next waymarker, turn right and keep going down until reaching some stones in a small clearing, where the track drops to the left at a right angle. The path then travels over a block of concrete embedded in the ground and turns left at another waymarker, continuing downhill to join the path at Pontycymer Lake.

This area is a Plant! wood, a Welsh Government scheme under which a tree has been planted to mark the birth or adoption of every child in Wales since 2008. The word 'plant' is also the Welsh word for child. A Cardiff schoolgirl came up with the idea, and the trees planted here include alder, common white birch, hazel and mountain ash.

Follow the path to the left and down the steps to the tarmac community route alongside the lake. There are some picnic tables here and just past these is the track heading back uphill to the Craig Barber memorial flag, which you can see from here. Follow the community route left for about a mile back to Parc Calon Lan, looking out for the wild horses that often graze here. Alternatively, as you walk upriver, you can cross one of several bridges to a parallel path on the other bank. The lakes and river lie directly next to the villages of Pontycymer and Blaengarw, where there are shops and cafés if you want to make a detour along the way.

Back at Parc Calon Lan, you can either keep to the left bank and walk around the lake and past the waterfall back to the car park, or you

The trail starts and ends in Parc Calon Lan

can cross the bridge just in front of the lake to enter the park itself. At the centre is a sculpture with the words of Calon Lan inscribed on it - can you read them?

The community route we've just returned along is very popular with cyclists and walkers. Heading south, it travels all the way down the valley to Bryngarw Country Park - which takes us nicely to Walk 20!

WALK 20

The Keepers' Trail

Bryngarw Country Park, Bridgend

Beneath this land a story sleeps...

The Keepers' Trail is a walk with a difference because you're in charge of deciding where to go – after all, no one likes being told what to do all of the time! More of a quest than a trail, this walk brings to life the diverse habitats of Bryngarw Country Park, unearthing some of its oldest secrets by finding and awakening the mythical Keepers, guardians of the magical Story of the Land. And there's good news for parents who spend a lot of time trying to lure their children away from screens and smartphones as this outdoor adventure is interactive, combining the best of both worlds!

Secrets wait to be unearthed at Bryngarw Country Park!
Photo by Daniel Lock

The Bryngarw Keepers were the idea of park ranger Dan Lock, who realised that a new way was needed to tell the story of Bryngarw and give visitors a richer experience of the natural landscape. With the help of a number of colleagues, particularly Bridgend's then tourism development officer Gina Gavigan, the project was designed to appeal to the imagination of visitors and uses sculpture, music and mythic storytelling to help reconnect with a sense of enchantment and mystery in the landscape.

The park is a 'mosaic' of habitats and unusual in south Wales in that it contains such a variety of environments within a relatively small space. The Keepers - seven-foot statues carved from 300-year-old Bryngarw oak - are the mythical guardians of the 'Story of the Land' and represent the 'spirit' of each area, including the river, the garden, the meadow and the woodland. But the Keepers have fallen asleep and must be awoken . . . only then will the ancient and forgotten Story of the Land be known once more!

Approx. distance	**As long as you want it to be!**
Approx. time	**See above!**
Starting point	**Bryngarw Country Park, Brynmenyn, Bridgend Grid ref: SS 9050 8541**
Grading	**An easy trail along mainly level paths, with extra care needed near water**
Suggested age	**Suitable for all ages**
Maps	**OS Explorer 166; OS Landranger 170**

Bryngarw Country Park is part of the Awen Cultural Trust and sits on the edge of Bridgend, at the foot of the Garw Valley. There's a small car parking charge but entry to the park itself is free. Note that the car park to use is the one in front of the visitor centre and not that next to Bryngarw House, which is now a country hotel and wedding venue.

From the visitor centre, explorers can obtain for free an old-style scroll map and a star talisman, their special key to the secrets of the land. The quest begins and ends at the Circle of the Keepers, another striking sculpture in the form of a flame, in front of the visitor centre. Pop your talisman into the audio box inside the flame and find out how, long ago, the keepers gathered here around the fire to tell their tales. You then have to use your map to explore the park and find each keeper, waking him or her by inserting your talisman and listening to their story...

The Keeper of the Meadow

On the hillside, away from the hustle and bustle of the visitor centre, is the meadow, a large grassland full of native wildflowers and bordered by ancient hedgerow. It's a tranquil space for play and relaxation, and surveying it all knowingly is the Keeper of the Meadow. Can you discover her story?

The Keeper of the Woodland

Bryngarw's woodland is as old as the hills, with mature sweet chestnuts, enormous beeches and, of course, the ancient oak from which the keepers were carved, meaning they were 'born and bred' on the land. Spring is the ideal time to visit, when the woods are transformed by bluebells, whilst in autumn it's a rainbow of red, yellow and burnt orange. Home to foxes, squirrels and woodpeckers, the woodland is full of mystery and mythical promise.

The Keeper of the River

The River Garw - or Afon Garw, meaning 'rugged river', in Welsh - runs from the hills north of Blaengarw to the Rivers Ogmore and

The Keeper of the River

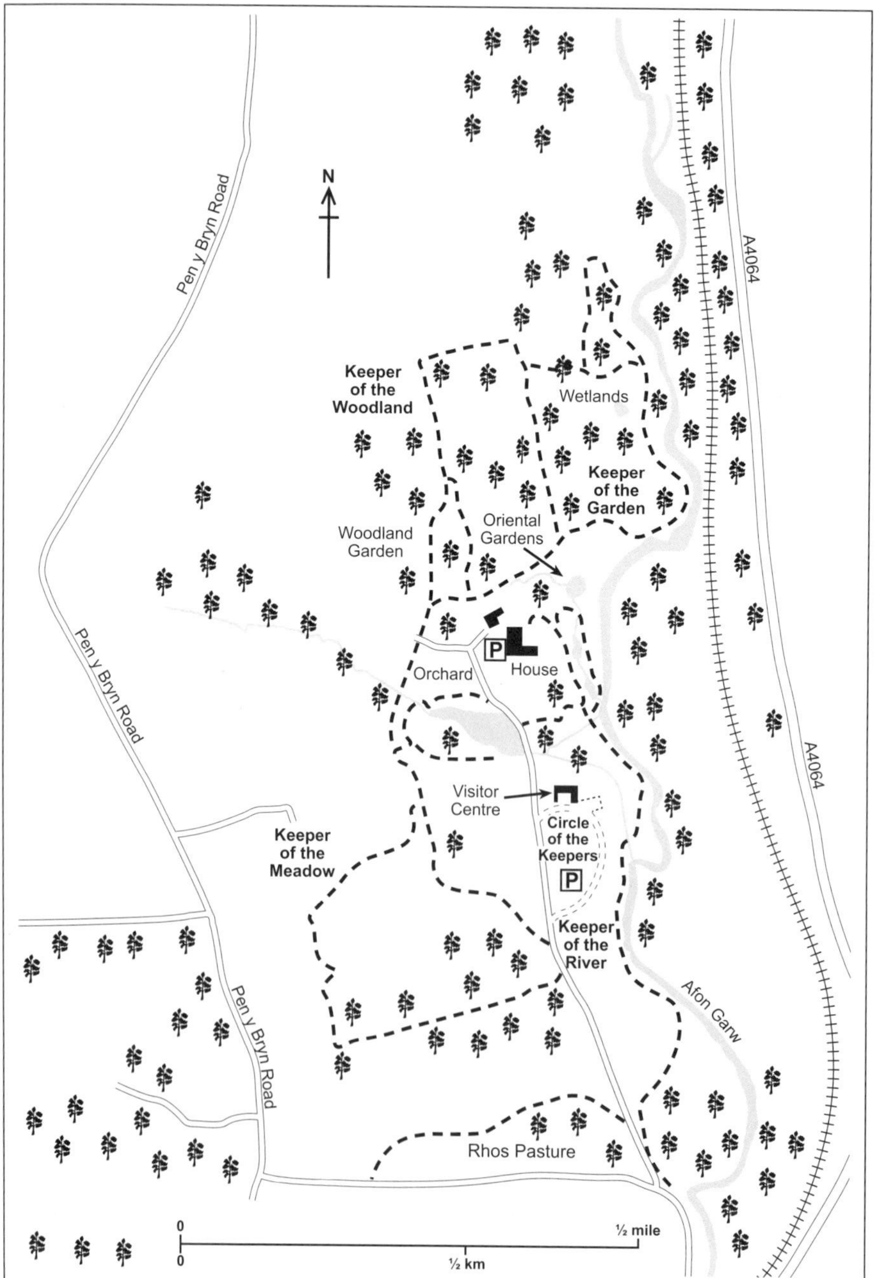
N
Pen y Bryn Road
Pen y Bryn Road
Pen y Bryn Road
A4064
A4064
Keeper of the Woodland
Wetlands
Keeper of the Garden
Oriental Gardens
Woodland Garden
House
Orchard
Visitor Centre
Circle of the Keepers
Keeper of the Meadow
Keeper of the River
Afon Garw
Rhos Pasture
0
½ mile
0
½ km

Llynfi. In the days of coal it was known as the 'black river' as it contained so much dust, but today it's much cleaner and flows peacefully past Bryngarw's rocky gorges. Look out for otters, dippers and kingfishers - and the Keeper of the River, of course!

The Keeper of the Garden

The formal garden is probably not what you expect to find on your hunt, looking as though it would be more at home in Japan than in the heart of a Welsh valley! The Oriental Garden was created more than 100 years ago by Captain Treharne, a wealthy man who once owned this lovely house and grounds. Every season different plants flower, from rhododendrons, magnolias and azaleas in spring and summer to fiery maples in autumn. A series of interlinking paths meets at the pond, where an ornamental bridge leads to a pretty, traditional teahouse. But where is the Keeper of the Garden?

The star talisman has six points, each numbered with Roman numerals and each activating a different part of the story. The sixth point is marked with a harp symbol and awakens the 'Song of the Keeper', a unique piece of music composed especially for the project and inspired by that particular habitat. Parents and grandparents usually enjoy the music as much as exploring children do!

When you have explored all four habitats, return to the Circle of the Keepers and insert your star one last time to finish your adventure. All explorers - now Keepers of the story themselves - receive a certificate from the visitor centre, where you'll also find Cedars Tearoom and a hearty selection of cakes and ice cream.

Finding the Keepers of the Land and hearing their stories will take some time but, if you're in no rush, there is plenty more to see and do in and around the country park. You could walk along the Garw Valley Trail - well, a section of it, at least! - an eight-mile national cycle route following a disused railway line from Bryngarw up into the valley, joining with other cycle and walking paths as it goes. There is also a series of shorter trails within the park boundaries, including the Riverside Ramble and the Meadow Meander, although you have probably already covered these tracks in your search for the keepers!

Next to the duck pond, where of course you can feed the ducks, is a fabulous play area containing the tallest slide we've found whilst creating this book. Have a go if you dare! There's also a picnic and barbecue area, as well as a clearing especially designated for building dens with any logs and branches you can find nearby.

This pretty teahouse is an unexpected sight in Wales!

Since their launch in 2014, the Keepers have rejuvenated Bryngarw and enabled hundreds of school children and families to unlock the story of the land. So enjoyable have visitors found the quest that Bridgend council's countryside and tourism team commissioned sculptor Dai Edwards to create a further 10 Keepers, which have been 'hidden' in different beauty spots throughout Bridgend. Do you remember the Keeper of the Pond at Kenfig National Nature Reserve in Walk 17? She is one of the new statues guarding the countryside and waiting to be found!

Take a look at **bridgendbites.com/doing** to find out more about the Nature Keepers and see how many more you can discover. The interactive content contained in the Dare to Discover app, such as poetry, images and videos, can only be seen when the user gets close to each keeper. The app has helped tourists and locals alike to discover Bridgend's green spaces and see new landscapes, from mountain valleys to golden beaches, and is a brilliant way of encouraging the next generation to look after the countryside.